WOMEN AND PARLIAMENT
1918-1970

Women and Parliament

1918-1970

Beverly Parker Stobaugh

An Exposition-University Book

EXPOSITION PRESS
HICKSVILLE, NEW YORK

45133

First Edition

© 1978 by Beverly Parker Stobaugh

All rights reserved, including the right of reproduction in whole or in part, in any form or by any means, electronic or mechanical, including photocopying, recording, or by any information storage and retrieval system. No part of this book may be reproduced without permission in writing from the publisher. Inquiries should be addressed to Exposition Press, Inc., 900 South Oyster Bay Road, Hicksville, N.Y. 11801

Library of Congress Catalog Card Number: 78-58555

ISBN 0-682-49056-3

Printed in the United States of America

Contents

45133

Tables

Chapter 6

Preface

This book evaluates the political development of British women as measured by election to Parliament. British women won both the right to vote and the right to stand for Parliament in 1918. Over the next fifty-two years, during which fifteen general elections were held, 570 women campaigned for seats in the House of Commons: ninety-four were successful. Statistics compiled on these 570 women candidates were analyzed through the use of a computer. Also tabulated were statistics for the male candidates who ran in three general elections (1929, 1945, and 1970) in order that relevant comparisons with women candidates might be made.

As examples of successful candidates, three remarkable women are presented: Katharine, Duchess of Atholl (Conservative); Ellen Wilkinson (Labor); and Eleanor Rathbone (Independent). Also, interviews with eight women candidates, both successful and unsuccessful, were conducted.

For the purpose of this study, the 570 women candidates were divided into two groups. Group I (which I designate as the "Pioneers") includes all women candidates in the seven general elections from 1918 to 1935; Group II (the "Moderns") includes all women candidates in the eight general elections from 1945 through 1970. The ten years that separate the Pioneers and the Moderns encompassed World War II, when no national elections took place.

A major conclusion of this study is that women were discriminated against by their parties. This discrimination is evident in the relatively few women selected by any major political party to stand for safe seats. Because political parties are more important to the British electorate than individual candidates, a candidate's constituency assumes tremendous importance.

The comparison of male and female candidates in the general elections of 1929, 1945, and 1970 illustrates the parties' discrimination against women. In these three elections, men were given proportionally many more safe seats to contest than were women. Only one-quarter of the women candidates were elected to Parliament; one-third of the men were elected. The women who were elected were, on the whole, better educated than their male counterparts, and had had more experience within their parties, and in local government. Statistics show that when given the opportunity to stand for a seat that might reasonably be expected to go to her party, a female candidate was likely to fare as well as a male candidate.

In comparing the two major parties. I found that the Conservatives have awarded their candidates a relatively higher proportion of safe seats than Labor and have had a higher percentage of winners. This, however, was more the case in the Pioneer period, when the Conservatives nominated more women to succeed their husbands than in the Modern period. In comparison with the Conservatives, Labor has selected more women to stand for election, has had more women win—often in elections in which the Conservatives won control of Parliament—and has appointed more women to ministerial posts. Regardless of party affiliation, a woman's political career was enhanced by working within her party, by holding public office on the local level, and by standing several times for national office.

During the Pioneer period, there was an upward trend in the number of women who ran for office in each general election. But during the Modern period—the last twenty-five years—the trend has been level. There is no indication that more women will run for Parliament in the near future, and there is no evidence that discrimination against women is lessening.

Introduction:
The Suffragist
Movement

In 1918 the long intense struggle of British women for political equality began to reach fruition. The Representation of the People Act that was passed in February gave the franchise to women thirty years old or older, if either they or their husbands owned property with an annual value of at least five pounds. In November of that same year, women twenty-one and over were granted the right to stand for Parliament, in the Qualification of Women Bill. And, finally, in 1928, *all* women twenty-one and over were given full voting privileges.

The femininist movement in Britain may have begun in 1792, with the publication of Mary Wollstonecraft's book *A Vindication of the Rights of Women*. Although it did not reach a wide audience, the book eloquently described the vicious circle of deprivation that surrounded upper- and middle-class British women. For these women, economic security depended on marriage to a prosperous man. Once married, a woman became the property of her husband. She had no rights over her property unless these were "secured to her by settlement";[1] that is, either through a prenuptial agreement or property in her name prior to marriage. Whatever money or property she acquired after marriage automatically belonged to her husband. No matter how he treated her, a wife could not divorce her husband; he, on the other hand, could obtain a divorce. For single women of the upper and middle classes, job opportunities were scarce. The few jobs that were considered respectable, such as work as a governess, were low paying. Neither high schools nor colleges were open to them. Politically, economically, and socially, they, like their married sisters, were second-class citizens.

In the nineteenth century, when the struggle for suffrage began, the only activities outside the home and family that were sanctioned for women of the middle and upper classes were those tied to charitable and philanthropic organizations. Opportunity for membership in the Birmingham Political Union and the Anti-Corn Law League, however, did enable women to become somewhat involved in activity of a more political nature. The former, composed mainly of working class people but including many middle-class members as well, approved the formation of a subsidiary Women's Political Association in 1839. Women were allowed to vote on resolutions but were not included in policy-making decisions. Although Chartists were concerned with political reforms, such as the secret ballot and universal manhood suffrage, they rebuffed attempts by member Joseph Sturge, a middle-class radical, to include suffrage for women among their principles. The Anti-Corn Law League was the center of middle-class political reform efforts, and women were allowed to participate. The two daughters of Richard Cobden and the brother of John Bright, both leaders of the League, later became active in the suffrage movement.

What happened in the nineteenth century that gave women the courage and staying power to fight for political and economic justice? At least one scholar attributes women's pursuit of freedom to a reaction against the confinement of the Victorian era.[2] Some scholars suggest that the French and American Revolutions were the catalysts in women's struggle for liberation. Others credit the Industrial Revolution with undermining the economic status of middle-class women with the introduction of factories and manufactured goods. These women were no longer needed for home production but they could not work in factories. The plight of working-class women who moved to the cities to work was only too visible. The destitution and misery of urban workers, intensified by the depression that followed the Napoleonic Wars, could not be as easily ignored as rural poverty, at least by people of conscience.

In the 1860s, the suffragist movement was becoming a political reality.[3] Composed mainly of middle-class women who had gone beyond their charitable works to attack social injustice on a national scale, the movement included a goodly number of writers and teachers.[4] Their first strategy took the form of an argument that women had the right to vote except where specifically forbidden in the Reform Bill of 1832, the first legislation that used the term "male enfranchise." This contention was based on a passage in the 1850 Act for Shortening the Language Used in the Acts of Parliament; namely, that the use of masculine form would automatically include both men and women unless otherwise stated. The suffragists also cited the tradition that women could participate in choosing knights of the shire for seats in Parliament.[5] They claimed that women's right to vote had been abrogated by custom, not law. But in the case of *Chorlton v. Lings*, tried in the Court of Common Pleas in 1868, the right of women to be placed on the Parliamentary Register (the list of qualified voters) was denied.

In 1865, feminists were encouraged by the election to Parliament of John Stuart Mill, an avowed advocate of women's suffrage. In 1866 they presented Mill with a petition for suffrage and in 1867 he proposed that an amendment for women's suffrage be attached to the Representative of the People Bill. This amendment would have substituted the word "persons" for "men" in the Reform Bill of 1832, thus granting voting rights to women for the first time. The unexpected number of supporting votes—74 for the amendment and 194 against—was cause for rejoicing.

In 1870, feminists had further cause to rejoice. The Liberal M.P. Jacob Bright offered a suffrage bill that actually passed its first reading. It was later rejected in committee, however. From 1870 to 1900, with the exception of 1874, a suffrage bill was proposed in every session of Parliament. In 1884, when William Woodall, Liberal M.P., proposed a suffrage amendment to the reform bill, supporters of suffrage were encouraged by the lack of unified resistance. But Prime Minister Gladstone refused to consider the amendment lest it endanger passage of the reform bill. In 1886, and again in 1897, a suffrage bill passed the first reading but failed in committee.

Parliamentary supporters of women's suffrage and those opposed used various strategems over the years between 1870 and 1918. The traditional method for changing the law was through the introduction of a "private member bill." These bills, however, had to survive several obstacles. First, an M.P. had to submit the bill to a ballot in order to secure a place on the agenda. Once given a place, the bill might still be kept from the floor if the time given to prior business was prolonged. Once presented, the bill might be "talked out"; that is, discussion could be purposely continued by opposing M.P.s until the time allotted for the bill's consideration was used up. A private member bill that did survive its first reading could be assigned by a hostile government to a committee of the whole House of Commons and left there to languish until the Parliamentary session ended. Bills to grant women voting rights were subjected to every one of these obstacles over the years.

Throughout Britain, the struggle to attain voting rights became a rallying point for feminists. The Sheffield Association for Female Franchise, the first of many local suffrage organizations, held its first meeting in 1850. The Manchester Women's Suffrage Committee was an early group that remained in existence until the struggle was won. It was founded in 1866 by Lydia Becker, who later served in London as editor of the *Women's Suffrage Journal* and became an expert on Parliamentary procedure. The most prominent suffragist organization in the second half of the nineteenth century was the London Society for Obtaining Political Rights for Women, formed in Kensington, London, in 1867 and later known as the London National Society for Women's Suffrage. Its members made immediate contact with Miss Becker's Manchester group and another new suffragist organization in Edinburgh.

In 1871, the London Society split into two groups. Some of the members, under the leadership of Josephine Gray Butler, were engaged in a crusade to repeal the Contagious Diseases Act, because of the law's discrimination against women. This bill had been passed as part of a campaign to combat venereal disease among military troops. It gave police the right to accuse any woman living within a specified area surrounding a military installation of prostitution; such a woman could therefore be forced to undergo periodic medical examinations. Because men within the installation were not also made to undergo mandatory medical examinations, the suffragists decried the double moral standard implied by the bill. Other members of the London Society did not back Mrs. Butler's activities, however. Despite their recognition of the merits of her cause, they were afraid that she was diverting attention from the primary focus of the movement, the franchise for women. They also feared that a struggle for the rights of prostitutes would alienate potential supporters of women's right to vote. Mrs. Butler and her followers withdrew from The London Society and formed the Central Committee of the National Society. Despite the split, there was no bitterness between the two groups. In 1882, they were merged under the leadership of Helen Blackburn. In 1883, the Contagious Diseases Act was suspended; it was repealed in 1886.

A significant breakthrough for all women was achieved in 1875 when Parliament passed a bill that allowed the traditionally male universities to admit women (although they were not compelled to do so). In the forefront of the struggle to obtain equal educational opportunities for women were Emily Davies and Elizabeth Garrett Anderson; the latter was the sister of Millicent Garrett Fawcett, another feminist leader. In 1877 when King's College and Queen's College of Physicians in Ireland opened their doors to women students, Elizabeth Anderson herself entered to become one of the first British women doctors. And in 1878 the Enabling Act gave a new charter to London University that, in effect, opened all its facilities to women. Not until 1920, however, was full citizenship in British universities offered women (Cambridge remained an exception).

By the turn of the century women could take advantage of several newly achieved opportunities. Middle-class women were entering careers in medicine, as both doctors and nurses, and in the British foreign missions. Working-class women were finding jobs in offices and factories as a result of the invention of the typewriter and the telephone—a new development that created a feeling of uneasiness amongst the labor unions. Receiving only subsistence wages and working desperately long hours in the still limited number of positions open to them, women were accused by the unions of taking work from men and keeping wages low.

In the eyes of the law, women were also achieving some rights. The 1857 Marriage and Divorce Act allowed wives to sue for divorce, although the grounds were more restricted than for husbands. The Married Women's Property Bill, passed in 1870, allowed women to control their own property. But a father still had the right to remove a child from its mother's care without providing just cause, and to determine his children's religion, what schools they would attend, and so forth.

Perhaps the most important early victories for women on the long road toward suffrage occurred in local government. In 1869 unmarried women who were property holders were granted the right to vote in municipal elections. A year later they won the right to vote and run for school board office. By 1894 district and parish councils were opened to them and in 1907 the last hurdle was cleared when they became eligible to vote and run for both county and borough councils. In spite of these victories, however, public interest in the suffrage movement began to wane in 1884, when Woodall's suffrage amendment in Parliament—originally given some hope of passage—did not gain a first reading.

Yet the dedicated band of suffragists did not weaken in resolve. And by the end of the century all the suffrage groups in Britain had been forged into one alliance, the National Union of Women's Suffrage Societies (N.U.W.S.S.).

As noted earlier, some members of the original London Society for Obtaining Political Rights for Women had formed a splinter group in 1871 called the Central Committee of the National Society. Although reunited in 1882, another split in the ranks accompanied the admission of women's groups formed to support the Liberal Party. Sixty-two women refused to accept a party alignment and, under the leadership of Lydia Ernestine Becker and Millicent Garrett Fawcett, they organized the Central Committee. Mrs. Fawcett's efforts were encouraged by her husband, Professor Henry Fawcett, a Liberal M.P. for Brighton. From this base, Mrs. Fawcett worked steadily over the next years to unite all suffrage organizations. By 1897 the N.U.W.S.S. was steadily recruiting members, holding public meetings, sending women on speaking tours, writing letters to the press, and publishing numerous pamphlets. Its goal was total enfranchisement for all women on the same basis as men.

Although in the early years of the movement, feminists sought to achieve the vote on the same terms as men—i.e., with property as the qualifying factor—they were disturbed that under the rules of coverture (legal status of married women) married women would be excluded from suffrage. This meant that only 300,000 to 400,000 unmarried women and widows would be allowed to vote. By 1903 all militant suffragists were demanding that both married and single women of property be enfranchised. By 1912, the more moderate suffragists followed suit.

As their numbers grew, suffragists worked actively during general elections for candidates of all parties who supported their cause. For their part, the political parties began to court women supporters ardently in 1883, when the Corrupt Practices Act was passed. This bill forbade the payment of salaries to the people (invariably men) who performed day-to-day political chores, such as canvassing, passing out literature, and arranging meetings. Now women volunteers were suddenly in demand. The parties began to organize auxiliary organizations for women. The Primrose League, "a Tory Militia," had many women associated with their efforts but only to give teas, not to contribute to policy decisions. Nor did it publicly support women's suffrage. The Conservative Party formed its first official Women's Council in 1885. In response, a Women's Liberal Federation was formed. This group was soon rent by dissension; some members, led by the Countess of Carlisle, refused to support any Liberal candidate who did not vow to support voting rights for women if elected. This splinter group formed the National Women's Liberal Association.

Although most suffragists tried to steer clear of identification with one party, a majority of Liberal candidates in the 1880s promised to support women's suffrage and were given active suffragist backing. Nevertheless, most Liberal M.P.s were ambivalent about the suffrage issue. Although they supported it in principle, their leaders opposed women's suffrage and all feared that, if given the vote, women of property would help to elect Conservative candidates. The Conservative Party, despite the potential benefits, opposed women's suffrage. Many individual Conservative M.P.s were sympathetic to the movement, however, but considered the issue of little importance and would not oppose their party's official position. Conservatives paid most attention to the issue when they were out of power (in 1886 and from 1892-95) and could use it to embarrass the Liberals.

Feminists who had expected Liberal Party support were enraged by the defection of the Liberal leader, W. E. Gladstone, in 1884. They believed that the amendment for a limited franchise for women proposed by Woodall in that year could have been added to the reform bill had Gladstone not vigorously opposed it. Voting with Gladstone were 104 Liberal M.P.s who had been counted as pro-suffragist.

Twenty-one years later, in 1905, when the Liberals formed a Government, a delegation of suffragists visited the Prime Minister, Sir Henry Campbell Bannerman, with high hopes of Liberal support for a franchise bill. The Prime Minister expressed his personal sympathy but refused to promise party support. When Sir Henry retired because of ill health, he was succeeded by H. H. Asquith (later first earl of Oxford and Asquith). For five years, Prime Minister Asquith prevented a suffrage amendment from reaching a vote, even though he made the issue an open one, allowing Liberal M.P.s to speak out as they wished rather than forcing them to follow the party position.

In 1910 an all-party committee of M.P.s drafted a conciliation bill, using the qualification of the municipal franchise (unmarried women who were property holders) to give women the vote. Lloyd George, Liberal Chancellor of the Exchequer, who had earlier supported suffrage, now opposed the bill. Although it reached a second reading, the Liberal Government would not give it facilities, and, as a result, it failed. The bill was rewritten, resubmitted in 1911, and again passed its second reading. Introduced on the floor of the House of Commons in 1912, it failed by only fourteen votes.

This close vote in 1912 was the result of several political decisions. First, Prime Minister Asquith had announced that a Government reform bill would be submitted in the next session of Parliament, and that a women's suffrage movement could be added then. Second, the Irish Nationalists who originally supported women's suffrage chose to withdraw their votes rather than to risk the loss of Asquith's support for Irish Home Rule. Third, many Labor M.P.s who supported the measure had been forced to return to their constituencies because a strike was in progress. Many people also blamed the furor caused by the actions of the most militant suffragists, who were then being arrested and imprisoned for their destruction of public property. After the failure of the conciliation bill in 1912, the suffragists were still hopeful that Asquith's Government reform bill would resolve the issue favorably. When the bill was presented, however, the Speaker of the House ruled that the government bill could not be amended to allow women's suffrage in its present form but must be rewritten and resubmitted in the next Parliament.

While the Liberals vacillated and the Conservatives opposed, the Labor Party supported suffrage for all adults from the very beginning of the suffrage movement. Yet it was not until 1912 that the National Union of Women's Suffrage Societies decided that its own best interests would be served by supporting Labor candidates. At about the same time, suffragists, thoroughly discouraged in their efforts at compromise, were themselves beginning to work for suffrage for all women, regardless of property qualifications.

Despite its commitment to equality of suffrage, the Labor Party had not been sympathetic to the organized suffragist movement because of its middle- and upper-class orientation. A struggle to extend the franchise to women who owned property had little appeal for them. Yet party men such as Keir Hardie, Philip Snowden, and George Lansbury, recognizing that it would be easier to open the door to all women if a privileged minority could first gain admission, supported suffragist activities.

Working-class women who joined the Labor Party had always been recognized as full party members. When the party rebuffed those suffragists who tried to gain Labor support—Millicent Fawcett and Emmeline Parkhurst—female leaders of the party were in accord with the decision. They viewed the suffragists as only peripherally involved with the main concerns of their own lives—better jobs and better pay for all workers. Only a few working-class women—e.g., Annie Kenney—were active in the movement.

Most working-class women worked outside the home for some portion of their lives. The jobs open to them were of the most boring sort and paid very little, usually in offices or factories where new machinery was being introduced. They had little time or money to contribute to the labor unions and they were virtually ignored by union organizers. As noted earlier, they were perceived as competing with working men for available jobs, were accused of keeping wages low, and, in addition, of being too passive or submissive to work for better conditions. There was another factor, too. As unskilled and often temporary workers, women were difficult to organize. In fact, the only group of women who were successfully unionized when women first entered the work force were workers in the cotton industry.

The Women's Protective and Provident League, founded in 1875 by Emma Patterson, was the first labor union organized solely for protection of women workers' rights. Mrs. Patterson herself had served as an apprentice to a bookbinder and was married to a cabinetmaker. Despite her working-class background, she believed that to form the League she would have to enlist the help of middle-class backers. In this she was successful, but the union was not accepted into the Trade Union Congress. After Mrs. Patterson's death in 1886, leadership passed to Lady Dilke, whose husband, Sir Charles Dilke, Liberal M.P., also supported the union and represented its interests in Parliament. In 1889 the name of the union was changed to the Women's Trade Union League. At the same time male organizers began to recruit women workers for this union. Finally, in 1903, when Mary Macarthur, wife of the chairman of the Labor Party (Will Anderson), became active in the League, it began to broaden its horizons.

Until she became an organizer, Mary Macarthur was employed by her father, a prosperous shop owner. An early feminist, she retained her maiden name when she married. Miss Macarther, upon joining the Women's Trade Union League, launched a drive to recruit male members. By 1905, the League membership had grown to 70,000, including 16,000 men.[6] By 1914 the League had 400,000 working women from the working and middle classes on its roles.

In 1906, Miss Macarthur turned away from the middle-class image so carefully cultivated for the League by her predecessor, Emma Patterson. She organized the National Federation of Women Workers (N.F.W.W.), a totally working-class union. The N.F.W.W. was open to all unorganized working women and to all those women in the trades who were being denied admission to male unions.

During World War I, women's place in the work force grew rapidly, bringing strength to women's unions. By 1918 there were more than one million organized women in Britain. The N.F.W.W. became part of the National Union of General Workers in 1919, and the Women's Trade Union League joined the General Council of the Trade Union Congress in 1921. In her role as leader of the Standing Joint Committee of Industrial Women's Organizations—a group representing all working women's organizations—Miss Macarthur was recognized nationally as the chief spokesman for working women's rights. Despite her identification with women's struggle for equality, she was not part of the suffragist movement.

As some of its critics observed, the suffragist movement was directed largely by middle-class women. Both working-class and upper-class members were in the minority. In fact, many upper-class women were actively opposed to the enfranchisement of women, signing antisuffrage letters and contributing articles to the journals. The Duchess of Atholl (whose Parliamentary career is described in chapter 5) made several speeches against enfranchisement.

The woman who brought a new passion and militancy to the women's movement as Britain entered the twentieth century also came from the middle class. She was Emmeline Pankhurst. Mrs. Pankhurst, as well as her husband, had been active for women's suffrage for many years before she became its most militant leader. (Dr. Richard Marsden Pankhurst, an attorney and an M.P., assisted the women's cause in the case of *Chorlton v. Lings* in 1868.) After her husband's death in 1898, Mrs. Pankhurst, the mother of five children, gave up her position as registrar of births and deaths in Manchester, to devote her full energies to the movement. Impatient with the moderate tone of the suffragists of her day, she and two of her daughters formed the Women's Social and Political Union (W.S.P.U.) in October of 1903—an organization whose militancy was reflected in its slogan, "Deeds, Not Words!" By 1911 the organization had three hundred branches throughout Britain.

In its early years, the W.S.P.U. included men and moderate women among its members; e.g., Mr. and Mrs. F. W. Pethick Lawrence and Charlotte French Despard. By 1913 the men and the moderates had departed, some to form new organizations—including Mrs. Pankhurst's daughter, Sylvia, who founded the East London Federation of the Suffragettes, a working-class organization. (Christabel, Mrs. Pankhurst's oldest child, was to remain by her mother's side throughout her militant career.)

Emmeline and Richard Pankhurst had at one time been active members of the Liberal Party, and Dr. Pankhurst had served as a Liberal M.P. But they left the party in 1884 when Gladstone refused to support a women's suffrage amendment. Later, while a member of the Manchester Suffrage Society, Mrs. Pankhurst and others tried to enlist the aid of Labor, but by 1900 she was disillusioned with that party, too. As leader of the W.S.P.U., she was opposed to whatever party was in power, because none supported her cause.

The W.S.P.U. at first devoted itself to many of the same activities undertaken by more moderate groups; i.e., recruitment and education. As time passed, however, its tone became stridently antimale, as well as antigovernment, and eventually members adopted confrontation with civil authorities as their primary tactic to focus national attention on their grievances.

The first confrontation occurred without planning. In October 1905, Christabel Pankhurst and Annie Kenney attended a political meeting in Manchester. Sir Edward Grey, a Liberal and a future Cabinet Minister, was the chief speaker; he and several other Liberals discussed the newly elected Government's plans. During the open discussion period, Misses Pankhurst and Kenney asked questions about the Liberal Government's stand on women's suffrage. When their questions were ignored, they repeated them again and again. Finally, they were forcibly evicted from the meeting by stewards. Arrested, they refused to pay fines and were jailed. A flurry of publicity attended the incident and the women's struggle received a new impetus. Mrs. Pankhurst and the W.S.P.U. decided to capitalize on the public's new awareness of their cause. They saw arrests and jailings as educational tools and sought to provoke the authorities by continued acts of civil disobedience.

By 1906 the W.S.P.U. had begun to step up its activities in London. At the beginning of each new Parliamentary session, members held a rally and then marched en masse to present the Prime Minister with a petition for women's suffrage. Invariably the marchers were scattered by policemen and many were arrested. Their trials received national publicity. As the number of arrests grew, many of the imprisoned militants went on hunger strikes. Their jailers used forced feedings to end their fasts—alienating broad segments of the public. Militant suffragists began to throw rocks at police and public buildings in order to add to the number of arrests.

In 1913 the Government passed the Prisoner's Temporary Discharge for Ill Health Act, immediately labeled the "Cat and Mouse Act." Under its terms, prisoners who refused to eat were to be released when their health was endangered and rearrested when their health improved. This was to continue until their prison terms had been served. In fact, few women actually served full terms, and many who attacked public property now sought to elude the police and escape arrest. While their activities did raise the public's consciousness, they also alienated moderates in the movement who abhorred violence and feared that the public might turn irrevocably against enfranchisement. Whatever their shortcomings, the militants forced Parliament to take the question of women's suffrage seriously; heretofore, it had been treated by many M.P.s as, at best, a minor issue and, at worst, a joke.

When World War I began, the women's movement entered a new phase. All suffrage groups suspended political activity, and the Government responded by granting amnesty to suffragist prisoners. Suffragists now devoted themselves to the war effort with the same zeal and dedication that had marked their struggle to win the vote. At first, the Government did not know how to put their energies to work. The women began to serve with the various relief organizations, having been well trained by their traditional roles in charitable organizations. Gradually, as their abilities were recognized, and the needs of war grew stronger, the Government hired women to staff their expanding offices. The military services created new women's auxiliaries. For the first time, women doctors and nurses were recruited to work in battle areas.

While middle-class women were being absorbed into the war effort in increasing numbers, working-class women were being thrown out of work. When the country went to war, the production of luxury items was severely curtailed, leaving large numbers of working women unemployed. Employers in industries producing strategic necessities resisted the hiring of women at first because the women were unskilled. But as women learned the necessary trades, employers enthusiastically recruited them. Now, working men saw their worst fears confirmed. In 1915 the trade unions forced the Government to agree that, when the war was over, women in the factories and offices would be made to give up their jobs to men returning from the military services. But during the war years women would receive wages equal to those earned by men.

As their skills and the need for their services increased, women heard their praises sung by the press and the public. The backbone of wartime industry, they were now encouraged rather than jeered. "Dazzled by their unwanted popularity, their high wages, and their interesting new work,"[7] their horizons and ambitions broadened, working women welcomed their new independence. And their rights and needs were not overlooked by the suffragists.

At the end of 1915, there was widespread speculation that the Government was preparing to establish a special register (a list of eligible voters). Suffragists informed the Government that they would not object if the register were simply to be used for preregistration. But if a change in the franchise for men was to be proposed, they demanded that women be included. An all-party conference was called, with the Speaker of the House of Commons as chairman; it was charged with the duty of writing a registration bill. The conference proposed that women who were householders or the wives of householders be given the right to vote in national elections. They suggested a minimum age of either thirty or thirty-five, to be decided by the full House of Commons.

All suffrage organizations that were still in existence met to discuss the proposal. They were insistent on an age minimum of thirty rather than thirty-five. Many women, however, were not happy with this high a minimum, because younger working women would thus be deprived of the protection afforded by the vote.

On February 6, 1918, the Representation of the People Act, granting the vote to women of thirty and over who were householders or married to householders, received the Royal Assent. On November 21, 1918, just three weeks before the general election, the Qualification of Women Bill was passed, allowing women twenty-one or over to stand for Parliament. Ironically, it was the antisuffragist Mr. Asquith who unintentionally eased the bill through the House of Lords. Weakened by his attack against them because of opposition to the budget proposed by Lloyd George, the House of Lords was in disarray and gave the Qualification of Women Bill no sustained opposition.

Following this breakthrough, the National Union of Women's Suffrage Societies, under the leadership of Millicent Fawcett, turned its attention to the extension of suffrage to all women twenty-one and over and to the political education of women. This latter objective was couched in the broadest terms, in order to satisfy those who saw the organization as a rallying point for all who sought to end political, social, and economic discrimination against women. The name of the organization was changed to the National Union of Societies for Equal Citizenship.

Ten years later—as early supporters of the movement had predicted —the door opened to a small number of women of property was broken down, and the vote and the right to stand for national office were extended to all adult women.

The women who met the challenges and responsibilities of full citizenship by standing for election to national office and serving in the House of Commons are the subject of this book.

        ❋   ❋   ❋

What were the characteristics of the women who entered national politics? In an effort to present an account of the political development of British women, as measured by their attempts to win national office, I have compiled statistics on the 570 women who ran for Parliament between 1918 and 1970. I have also tabulated statistics for the male candidates who won in three general elections (1929, 1945, and 1970), in order to present relevant comparisons. These statistical analyses are contained in chapters 4-6. The data came from a variety of published sources, as discussed in the Appendix.

But the statistics fall short in portraying the human side of the story. So I supplemented these statistical analyses with interviews of eight women selected to represent a cross section of successful and unsuccessful candidates, from each of the major parties, during different time periods. These women helped not only by discussing their own careers but also by describing their contemporaries.

To present a more comprehensive picture of the women in Parliament, I present biographical sketches of three women, chosen to exemplify class attitudes toward the suffragist movement. *Katharine, Duchess of Atholl,* Conservative M.P. from 1923 to 1938, was an upper-class woman, who received little formal education. She actively opposed suffrage for women and, in fact, made speeches in opposition before 1918. *Ellen Cicely Wilkinson,* Labor M.P. from 1924 to 1931 and 1935 to 1947, was raised in a working-class home, but because of her considerable abilities, won several scholarships that enabled her to acquire a college education. As interested as she was in the issue of suffrage, however, she was more concerned about class rather than sex discrimination. *Eleanor Rathbone,* Independent M.P. from 1929 to 1946, came from a financially secure middle-class background. She attended Oxford before women were accepted as full members of the institution, was an active suffragist, and throughout her Parliamentary career was interested in all issues relating to women's rights. As all three women are deceased, information came from a variety of unpublished and published documents.

Part One:

THREE REMARKABLE WOMEN

1

The Duchess
of Atholl

Elected in 1923 to represent the Scottish district of West Perthshire and Kinross, the Duchess of Atholl, a Conservative, was the first Scottish woman to sit in the House of Commons. She was then forty-nine years old and would serve in Parliament for the next fifteen years.

Before 1918, Katharine Marjory Ramsay Atholl had been no advocate of suffrage for women. Indeed, she had appeared at many antisuffrage meetings to declare that women were not ready for the vote, that they needed more political experience. Clearly, she did not include herself in this caveat. And, in fact, she was no stranger to politics. Her husband, George Stewart-Murray, had served as Unionist (Conservative) M.P. from West Perthshire for ten years before entering the House of Lords in 1917 as the eighth Duke of Atholl. When, in 1905, his first attempt to enter Parliament had been unsuccessful, Katharine had decided that the Unionists had not given him sufficient backing. To prevent this from happening again, she joined the Perthshire Women's Unionist Association and, in 1907, became its president.

When the Duchess entered Parliament, her concerns were fairly well determined by her upper-middle-class background and aristocratic marriage. Before her eventual defeat in 1938, the scope of her interests had become international. Her devotion to the Republican cause during the Spanish Civil War and her ceaseless campaign to alert Great Britain to the threat of Fascism made her a national figure. She was admired by politicians such as Winston Churchill for recognizing the dangers of German aspirations for world conquest, denounced by others as "the Red Duchess," a Communist sympathizer.

✿   ✿   ✿

Katharine Marjory Ramsay was born in 1874 into an old East Perthshire family, the Ramsays of Bamff, who could trace their ancestors back to the thirteenth century. On her mother's side, she was related to the Stewarts of Ardovorlich in West Perthshire. Katharine was one of

3

eight children, and the oldest of her father's five children by his second marriage.[1]

The Ramsays lived a comfortable, quiet life. During the ten months of the year that they lived in Bamff, Katharine's father devoted his time to the study of history. (He was the author of a history of England.) Katharine's three older half-sisters tutored all five younger children at home. In August and September, the family vacationed at the summer resort of St. Andrews. This tranquil pattern was changed somewhat in 1887 when the Ramsays moved to London, in order that the children might receive a more comprehensive education.

Katharine proved to be a particularly good student, and at the age of seventeen was offered a scholarship to one of the women's colleges at Oxford. Because music was her major interest, however, she elected to study at the Royal College of Music. For the next four years she studied the piano. Several poems by Robert Louis Stevenson that she set to music were published as a book, but Katharine viewed her talent as a social rather than a professional asset. She ended formal studies at the age of twenty-one.

Katharine and her mother were in constant demand for evening entertainment on their frequent visits to the country homes of friends, Katharine at the piano accompanying her mother's singing. It was during such a visit, in 1896, that she met her future father-in-law, the seventh Duke of Atholl, Chieftain of all the Murrays. The Duke invited Katharine and her mother to visit his home, Blair Castle, for the Atholl Gathering. There, Katharine met the Duke's older son, Tullibardine, called Bardie by his family and friends. Throughout the following year, Katharine and Bardie corresponded and, occasionally, met. By June of 1897 they were engaged, though they chose not to announce their engagement formally so that Bardie could serve with General Kitchener in the Sudan campaign. He left for Egypt in January of 1898, but before the end of the year he had contracted typhoid fever and was forced to return to England. On July 20, 1899, he and Katharine were married at St. Margaret's, Westminster.

On their return to the family home of Blair Atholl after their European honeymoon, Katharine and Bardie were greeted by their tenants according to tradition. After their health was toasted, "and about halfway up the long front approach at Blair, the horses were taken out, and relays of men dragged the carriage to the Castle."[2] Thus began a "partnership" that both Katharine and Bardie assumed would conform to the comfortable aristocratic pattern of the late nineteenth century. For families like theirs, socially and financially secure, even war did not bring untoward discomfort. Though Bardie served in the Boer War and the tragic Gallipoli campaign of World War I, they were not separated. Katharine followed her husband to South Africa and to Egypt. During both tours of duty, she organized entertainments for wounded troops.

In 1917, the seventh Duke of Atholl died. Bardie and Katharine discovered that he had left the estate in debt and that they would be forced to exercise some domestic economies. Nevertheless, the tranquil pattern of their everyday life was not disturbed. Bardie served as Lord-Lieutenant of Perthshire, continued his interest in sports, and worked to establish a Scottish National War Memorial Museum in Edinburgh Castle. Katharine took part in the activities of several committees. By 1928, however, continued financial difficulties forced them "to sell a lot of land, the best of the family jewellery, and the lease of a corner house in Eaton Place."[3] Nevertheless, the family retained over 200,000 acres of their land.[4]

In her autobiography, the Duchess attributed the family's financial difficulties to the influx of low-priced Russian timber. According to the Duchess, the use of slave labor made it possible for Russia to export its timber at "below cost," creating an unfavorable market for Scottish timber.

The eighth Duke of Atholl's unsuccessful plan to produce houses made from steel for his tenants, and unprofitable investments in a Jamaican sugar estate, further depleted his inheritance. In 1932, he and Katharine found it necessary to set up a private company to take control of the Atholl inheritance—the land, Blair Castle, and the family heirlooms. A personal friend, Annie, Lady Cowdray, bought the controlling shares in the company and the Duke was elected chairman. But "inevitably, all effective control passed from his hands."[5]

Six years after their marriage, in 1905, Bardie had entered politics. As mentioned earlier, his first campaign as the Unionist candidate from West Perthshire was unsuccessful. The family's large land holdings were unquestionably a political handicap. Landless farmers in the district particularly resented his use of a portion of his land for a deer forest. To defuse this issue, Bardie invited four members of the Liberal Party, four Unionists, and two nonparty men to join him in a tour of the Atholl deer forest, an area of some thirty square miles. Convinced by what they saw that the land was unsuitable for farming, the nine men signed a formal statement to this effect that was widely circulated within the electoral district. When Bardie ran again for the West Perthshire seat in 1910, he won, by the narrow margin of 300 votes. He held the seat for seven years. Upon the death of his father in 1917, he resigned from the Commons and entered the House of Lords.

Bardie's election in 1910 meant that the family had to divide its time between Scotland and London. Nevertheless, Katharine continued to serve on several committees. She had become president of the Perthshire branch of the British Red Cross Society in 1909 and would hold that post until 1945. In 1912, she was appointed to a governmental committee formed to investigate medical service in the Scottish Highlands. She also served, in 1917 and 1918, on a governmental committee that examined the living conditions of the Scottish Tinkers (gypsies). She was commandant of the Blair Castle Auxiliary Hospital from 1917 to 1919; vice chairman of the Association of Education Authorities in Scotland from 1919 to 1924; and chairman of the Scottish Board of Health's Consultative Council for Highlands and Islands from 1920 to 1924.

After World War I, Bardie was named Lord Chamberlain to King George V. He and Katharine made many friends among the members of the diplomatic corps and were more in touch with international politics than heretofore. One of their closest friends was the Spanish ambassador, Merry del Val. In her autobiography, however, the Duchess did not indicate that this friendship was in any way responsible for her activity during the 1930s on behalf of the Republican government of Spain.

Six years after the Duke of Atholl left the House of Commons, Sir James Wilson, chairman of the Unionist Association in Crieff, asked the Duchess to stand as the Unionist candidate for Parliament for West Perthshire and Kinross. Her winning margin in the election of 1923 was half that of her husband's in his first winning campaign—150 votes from an electorate of 25,000. When she took her seat in that year, there were only six other women with her in Parliament: an independent, three from the Labor Party, and two others from the Conservative Party.

Parliamentary Career: 1924-1938

Shortly after she was sworn in, in January of 1924, the Duchess gave a victory speech to the Joint Committee of Edinburgh Women's Organizations. She discussed women in politics.

> I think we have still to try to make the House of Commons and the Nation realise what women can contribute to the work of Parliament. To do this we have to use many of the qualities we find needed in our domestic life. Forty years ago, the ideal wife was one who said "Amen" to her husband whenever he opened his mouth. Today that idea has been abandoned, and we have instead an ideal comradeship of partnership in life's happiness and difficulties alike, which we recognize as much better.[6]

Her new role as an M.P. was not an improvement for her socially. When the King opened Parliament on January 15, 1924, she stood amongst a large group of Parliamentary members with only a glimpse of the proceedings. Previously, she had always been present at the ceremony formally dressed and seated with a clear view of the King as well as those of the entire assembly.

Within the year, the Duchess was forced to campaign again, in the general election of October 1924. The Conservative Party captured this election, and the Duchess won her seat by more than 8,000 votes. During her first term, her interests were restricted to what were traditionally labeled as feminine issues, e.g., the guardianship of infants and women's suffrage. She worked to have the vote extended to women upon their twenty-first birthday, since the Representation of the People Act of 1918 applied to women only when they reached the age of thirty. After the Conservative win in 1924, she was appointed by Prime Minister Baldwin to a ministerial post, Parliamentary Secretary to the Board of Education, reporting to Lord Eustace Percy. She held this post until 1929. Although it was a great honor to become the first Conservative woman (and only the second woman)[7] to hold ministerial rank, the position itself was an unimportant one. Her duties consisted primarily of awarding prizes at schools throughout Great Britain on Prize Day. She wrote that as a woman Parliamentary Secretary she was a "novelty" and "fair game as distributor of prizes."[8] In 1926 her duties were expanded when the Canadian Educational Council made arrangements for her to visit Canada to discuss educational problems with members of the provincial governments.

In 1926, Sir Austen Chamberlain, Foreign Secretary, invited the Duchess to join the delegation to the annual League of Nations meeting in Geneva. There she worked on two committees, one that studied welfare and morals, and the other, the education of youth. She also received recognition from other sources, for she was awarded honorary degrees from McGill University, Columbia University, and Oxford University. She even had a ship named after her, *The Duchess of Atholl*.

In the general election of 1929, the Duchess retained her seat by a margin of more than 3,000 votes, although the Labor Party won the election. With the loss of her ministerial post she turned to other tasks. She and Colonel Josiah Wedgwood organized an all-party committee to investigate the practice of circumcision for girls in the British colonies in Africa. Representing the committee, she attended an international Save the Children meeting in 1931. There she met Jomo Kenyatta for the first time. "He spoke excellent English," she later wrote, "but there was something very unsympathetic about him."[9]

Gradually, the Duchess broadened her political activity. To study the question of extending more power to the provincial governments in India, she organized an India Study Group, serving for two years as honorary secretary under the chairmanship of Sir Reginald Mitchell Banks. Eventually she came to oppose all transfer of power from the central government of India to the provincial bodies and supported Winston Churchill in his position on this issue. Her opposition was based on two concerns. She feared a conflict between the Hindus and the

Moslems, and, perhaps more important, she wanted British trade in India to be protected. With the passage of the India Bill in 1935, she felt her cause was lost.

Although her concerns were usually humanitarian—raising the allowance paid to unmarried mothers, providing education for children living on canal boats—she did not hesitate to vote as her concern for British economic strength dictated. Thus, in 1936, she voted against the Government Education Bill, which would have raised the minimum age for leaving school from fourteen to fifteen. "Industry needs children of that age," she said. Denouncing her vote, Lady Astor declared: "If the Duchess of Atholl had her way, English children would still be up the chimneys and down the mines."[10]

In the early 1930s, the Duchess accepted the chairmanship of a subcommittee formed by Conservative M.P.s to investigate Russian trade. At about this time, the government published an official document, called the "Russian Blue Book," which purported to describe prevailing conditions in Russia. Determined to publicize the political and economic climate in Russia, the Duchess began to meet with refugees from that country. In 1931 she wrote *Conscription of a People*, in which she criticized the British government for extending credit to Russia and proposed that all sales of arms and machinery to Russia be terminated.[11]

The Duchess also joined the Christian Protest Movement, founded by Canon Gough to publicize the persecution of religious believers within Russia. In the spring of 1936, however, she lost her position as one of three presidents of the organization, probably as a result of her efforts to expose religious persecution in Germany.[12]

From the time of Adolf Hitler's seizure of power in Germany, the Duchess of Atholl recognized that the Fascists were the greatest threat to world security. She read a translation of *Mein Kampf* as soon as it appeared in England and was dismayed to learn from a German scholar that the English copy had omitted Hitler's most vitriolic and aggressive statements. When German troops entered the Rhineland, the Duchess supported Winston Churchill in his pleas for a strong stand against German aggression. She had come to believe that Germany, under Hitler, was a far greater menace to Great Britain than was Russia.

In November 1936, the Duchess made her first foreign policy speech in the Commons. She urged that Britain give its support to Czechoslovakia, Yugoslavia, and Rumania in their struggles to withstand German invasion. She stated that these three nations needed to be reassured that the League of Nations would not abandon them. Later, after a visit to the three countries at the invitations of their governments, she wrote that Europe was "trembling in the balance between dictatorship and democracy."[13]

In the 1930s, the Duchess was aware that her growing preoccupation with foreign affairs might endanger her political career. She was, however, not "unmindful of home affairs," she wrote, and even "scored a minor triumph when I managed to secure the admission of gamekeepers to the benefits of national insurance."[14] Nevertheless, for the election of 1932, she made foreign affairs the main theme of her campaign. Although she retained her seat, her advisors warned that "most listeners would have liked to hear more about home affairs."[15]

With the advent of the Spanish Civil War, the Duchess turned her total attention and effort to the cause of the Spanish Republicans. At a time when the British government tended to be sympathetic to Franco and the average English voter was primarily interested in staying out of the war, the Duchess attempted to arouse Great Britain and the world to the dangers of Fascism in Spain.

In the 1930s, England was purchasing one-half of all Spain's exports and supplying one-fifth of its imports. Furthermore, a great deal of English money was tied up in investments in Spain.[16] Although the government was willing to participate—with Russia, Germany, Italy and Portugal—in the Non-Intervention Committee established in response to Republican claims of Fascist support for Franco, the committee's operations were superficial and ineffectual. Supporting Winston Churchill, the Duchess urged the government to take the problem of intervention to the League of Nations. But England stayed on the sidelines. The fear of a divided nation—torn between anti-Fascist and anti-Communist factions—kept the government locked into an uneasy neutrality.

The Duchess became more and more involved in her crusade to bring aid to the Republicans. In *Searchlight on Spain,* she chronicled the sources of unrest that led to the Civil War: the failure of the Spanish monarchy and the Spanish Catholic Church to respond to the distress of the landless peasants and urban industrial workers. She attributed the violent uprisings that followed the 1931 election of the Republican government to the Anarchists and Fascists. Unlike many other observers, she denied the existence of a Communist threat to Spanish stability. Talk of a Communist takeover in 1936 was, she insisted, the smokescreen thrown up to protect Franco, who had promises of help from Mussolini in his attempt to establish a dictatorship. The introduction of Fascist forces from Germany and Italy into the Spanish struggle alarmed the Duchess to such a degree that she was unable to recognize the Communists' role in undermining the Republican government, their attempts to destroy all political opposition under the guise of anti-Fascist activity.

The Duchess proposed that the Spaniards be left to fight their civil war without interference, certain that a Loyalist victory would be the result, bringing with it "a new hope of peace for Europe."[17] Her greatest fear was that a Franco victory would mean the expansion of Fascist influence in Spain. Franco would be "unable to refuse [Italy and Germany] the use of ports and air bases in event of war."[18] A Fascist Spain would endanger Gibraltar, as well as British ships in the Mediterranean, and, in the event of a war with Germany and Italy, France would be forced to defend a third frontier.

The Duchess's concerns about the Spanish Civil War were not all political. When a group of M.P.'s organized an All-Party Committee for Spanish Relief, she became its chairman. Serving with her were Eleanor Rathbone and Lord Listomel as vice-chairmen, and Wilfred Roberts as honorary secretary.[19] The purpose of the committee was to transfer Spanish children from bombed areas to safer towns in Spain, and to establish a means of sharing information between existing relief organizations. The Duchess and Eleanor Rathbone also formed the Basque Children's Committee, which brought 4,000 Basque children from Bilbao to England in May of 1937. They lived in a camp set up for them on a thirty-six-acre tract in Southampton.[20] The children were chosen without regard to their parents' political loyalties, but questions were raised in the press and in Parliament about a possible violation of the British policy of nonintervention.[21] Many M.P.s argued that the children should be returned to Spain at once. The Committee, however, would return a child only after receiving a request from its legitimate parents. By July of 1937 only one child had been returned, but another 160 were to be returned to Spain in November. There had been no communication with the parents of the remaining children.[22]

In order to appraise the situation at first hand, and, more particularly, to assist in the organization of relief for the wounded, the Duchess, Eleanor Rathbone, Ellen Wilkinson, and Dame Rachel Crowdin visited the Republican areas of Spain—Barcelona, Valencia, and Madrid—for ten days, in April, 1937.[23] In Valencia the Duchess was taken by government representatives to buildings housing Italian prisoners. The prison was clean, well lit, and adequately ventilated; the prisoners well fed and comfortably clothed. The visitors assumed that Republican prisons were the same everywhere, never questioning whether their tour was selective. Many observers were understandably cynical about the Duchess's naiveté. George Orwell, who was serving in the Republican army in Barcelona at the time, wrote that the Duchess "did not really believe in the existence of anything outside of the smart hotels." He wondered if her hosts were able to find "some butter for the Duchess of Atholl."[24]

While in Madrid, the Duchess made a radio address to foreign nations, asking for help for Spanish children.[25] In Paris on her return trip, she stated in a press interview that Republican prisoners were well treated and well fed. She also discussed the insurgents' indiscriminate bombing and strafing of women and children.[26] Despite the fact that, as a representative of a neutral government, she was on dubious ground in making political statements, there seems to have been no adverse reaction in Britain to her public expressions.

The Duchess also joined the Dependent Aid Committee organized by Charlotte Haldane to help the families of British volunteers in Spain. Mrs. Haldane and her staff were all avowed Communists, yet the Duchess seemed unaware of the embarrassment that this association might involve. There were, in fact, many prominent non-Communist sponsors for the committee, including Clement Attlee. In July, 1938, however, several M.P.s accused the committee of engaging in illegal activity—recruiting troops for the International Brigade. The Duchess, as a member of the government and a member of the committee, denied the allegations. She did admit, however, that outsiders had gained access to the committee's office and may have used information stolen from committee files.

Perhaps the Duchess's major contribution to the Republican cause in Spain was her book, *Searchlight on Spain,* one of the most widely read books of the time. She was also active in fund-raising attempts for the Republican cause and for this purpose visited the United States in 1938. Britons who resented her partisanship labeled her a Communist sympathizer and referred to her as "Red Kitty" or "the Red Duchess."

For the Duchess, the threat of Fascism to the security of the Western world overshadowed all other political issues in the 1930s. Despite her earlier distrust of Russia, she was now convinced that internal conditions in that country had vastly improved and that the Spanish Communists were "fighting for National independence and for the defense of the democratic Republic."[27]

The Duchess worked hard to convince Parliament that Britain should arm and should honor its commitments to the smaller states in Europe as well as France. She believed that with strong support from France and England, the League of Nations could turn back Fascist aggression and avert war. (Although she urged the government to arm and to begin conscription, however, she refused to vote additional taxation on the wealthy. When money was needed, she believed, wealthy Englishmen would contribute.) Her ultimate goal was a peaceful, economically secure British nation.

As late as 1936, the Duchess was still addressing herself in the Commons to issues such as agriculture, education, and unemployment. In 1937, however, eighteen of the twenty debates in which she actively participated were concerned with foreign affairs. Sixteen dealt directly with Spain, Germany, and Italy. In 1938, only four out of forty-three entries dealt with internal affairs. But her interest in international issues was never fully accepted by her constituents. On November 15, 1937, three members of the executive council of the Perthshire Unionists

Association resigned "because they did not agree with the views of the Duchess of Atholl, M.P. for the constituency, on the Spanish war."[28] Yet no action was taken by the Association against the Duchess because the Association had previously agreed that she was a free agent.

On April 29, 1938, the Duchess resigned her position as Government Whip "on account of the failure of the government to take adequate steps to secure the withdrawal of Italian troops from Spain, or to take action with other Powers to safeguard peace in Central Europe and on the shores of the North Sea."[29] She had adopted the same course in 1935 over the India Bill and had suffered no political consequences. But in November 1938, the Unionist Association in her district "decided by a majority to seek a candidate other than the Duchess of Atholl, M.P., for the next election in the constituency." This action was based on her refusal to support "the Prime Minister's policy of peaceful understanding in Europe."[30]

The Duchess immediately resigned from Parliament. She decided to run as an Independent in the by-election, on a platform of opposition to the foreign policy of Prime Minister Chamberlain. The Liberal candidate, a Mrs. MacDonald, chose to ignore foreign policy issues, and to attack the Duchess on the domestic front. "The Duchess of Atholl has no land policy," she said, "and Scotland is suffering from neglect just as much as Spain is suffering from bombs."[31] The Duchess responded that she would fight the by-election "on foreign policy and national defense, dealing with agriculture because it is our main industry in the constituency and an important part of national defense."[32]

Some members of the Liberal Party, who wanted the Chamberlain government defeated on any grounds, advocated that the party support the Duchess. This outlook prevailed, and on December 9, 1938, Mrs. MacDonald withdrew from the race.

The Unionist Association selected a forty-two-year-old farmer named W. McNair Snadder as its candidate. His position was clear: there is "no shadow of doubt at all in my mind," he said, "that Mr. Chamberlain is leading us along a road of hope . . . no great nation [Germany] could be kept in perpetual humility or with a sense of being thwarted."[33]

During the campaign the Duchess had to fight charges that she was a Communist. She was sent fake telegrams, signed "Stalin," with the message: "Greetings from Moscow." Rumors were circulated that the Communist party was supporting her candidacy. The Unionist candidate, Mr. Snadder, was called a Fascist in some quarters and was forced to state in public that he was neither a Roman Catholic nor a Fascist.

Many prominent men and women rallied to the Duchess's cause: Captain Liddell Hart, military correspondent for *The Times,* the Dean of Chichester, Maynard Keynes, Dr. W. W. Seton-Watson, Lady Violet

Bonham Carter, Lord Cecil, and Wilfred Roberts. Her colleague Eleanor Rathbone "gave what support she could to the lost cause."[34] Winston Churchill sent encouraging messages: "Your victory as an Independent member adhering to the first principles of the Conservative and Unionist Party can only have an invigorating effect upon the whole impulse of Britain's policy and Britain's defence."[35]

The campaign was strenuous. Her district, one of the largest in Great Britain, was eighty miles long and sixty-five miles wide, yet at that time the average population was ten people per square mile. It was estimated that one-half of the electorate heard one or both of the candidates during the campaign. Although the Duchess had the advantage of being the incumbent, her campaign organization was poorly run, and, despite predictions that she would carry the election, she went down to defeat. *The Times* of London headlined the story of her loss as "Encouragement to Mr. Chamberlain."[36]

Both *The Times* and the *Annual Register*[37] attributed the loss to her overriding interest in foreign affairs. To the voters in this rural area, agricultural problems were more important. The fact that the Duchess was a woman and a wealthy aristocrat did not endear her to her agrarian constituents. The support she had received from them in earlier campaigns had been largely due to the efforts of James Paton, now President of the Unionist Association in Perthshire. When she broke with the Chamberlain government, she lost his backing.

The Duchess had also alienated many of her women supporters with her stand against Fascism. They called her a "warmonger" because of her "query of the Munich settlement."[38]

With the loss of her seat in Parliament, the Duchess's political career ended. She lived in semiretirement on her Scottish estate until her death in 1960, long enough to have her predictions of the dangers of Fascism vindicated. During her last years, she attempted to alert her countrymen to the worldwide menace of Communism.

During her tenure in Parliament, the Duchess of Atholl did much to dispel any illusions that women in government would be content to confine themselves to "women's issues." As she gained experience, her horizons broadened, and she risked her political career to alert her nation to the dangers that the majority preferred to ignore. In January of 1924, as she began her first term in the Commons, she had declared: "We have still to try to make the House of Commons and the Nation realize what women can contribute to the work of Parliament." Whatever her failings—mainly an unwillingness to recognize some of the complexities of international politics—she operated in the political arena with skill, conviction, and courage.

Conclusion

The Duchess of Atholl's career exemplifies the concerns of the women who were Pioneer Conservative M.P.s. Although she had opposed the Suffragist Movement, she accepted the Conservative party's offer to stand for her husband's seat. Once in Parliament, she tended to follow her party's policy and was not dedicated to any personal program. Thus, her break with the Conservative Party, caused by her support for the Spanish Liberals, was a surprising occurrence; few M.P.s—men or women—supported their ideals to such an extent.

2
Ellen Wilkinson

Ellen Cicely Wilkinson, daughter of working-class parents, was the only Labor woman candidate elected to Parliament in the General Election of 1924. She is typical of the Labor "pioneers" elected to Parliament before 1945. She was a dedicated Socialist and devoted her life to improving the conditions of workers throughout the world. Although not a militant, she was an ardent feminist.

Miss Wilkinson served nineteen years as an M.P. from 1924 to 1931 and from 1935 to 1947. In 1924 she was elected to represent the large industrial constituency of Middlesborough. Only thirty-three years old at the time, she was a successful trade union organizer and had already been elected to the Manchester City Council. After serving as M.P. for seven years, she was defeated in the General Election of 1931. Four years later, she returned to the House of Commons to represent the depressed industrial area of Jarrow, a seat she retained until her untimely death in 1947.

This tiny red-haired dynamo has yet to be discovered by biographers, an oversight perhaps due to a lack of personal papers. The only records of her political career that bear her own touch are a series of personal scrapbooks containing newspaper clippings, to be found in the Labor Party Library in the Transport House in London.

✿　　✿　　✿

Ellen Wilkinson was born in Manchester on October 8, 1891. Her father, Richard Wilkinson, had been a cotton operative and was, at the time of her birth, an insurance agent. Although he never earned more than $16 a week, he was a Conservative and began voting Labor only at the insistence of his daughter. Money was always short for the Wilkinsons, and they lived in "one of those dreary little houses which make up the streets of Manchester," yet three of the four children, the two boys and one of the girls, received college educations, and "the family never went short of good food and clothes and annual holidays."[1] We get a poignant insight into Miss Wilkinson's early years from an incident described by Edith, Lady Summerskill. She talked of her colleague's wistful comment when, looking up at the tall Summerskill boy, she referred to her own five-foot stature and said, "I'd be tall like you if I had had plenty of milk when I was a baby."[2]

Miss Wilkinson's education began in a neighborhood school in Ardwick, a town within the borough of Manchester. She attended the Stretford Road Secondary School, and, with the aid of scholarships, she entered Owens College at Manchester University, where she received an M.A. degree with honors in history. When she was nineteen she was awarded the Jones National History Scholarship.

Miss Wilkinson joined the Labor Party while still in school. She told of attempting to register for a political debate and discovering that both the Liberal and Conservative positions were already taken. Although a Liberal at the time, she decided to argue for Labor in order to participate. So skillful was her presentation that she won the debate and in the process made at least one convert—herself.[3] In 1912 she joined the Independent Labor Party.

After graduation from the university, Miss Wilkinson taught school for a short time. In 1912 she became the election organizer for the National Union of Women's Suffrage Societies, a job that ended two years later at the outbreak of World War I. Miss Wilkinson was ambivalent about the declaration of war, because the suffragists were loyal supporters of the government, but the Women's International League, in which she was active, opposed the war. She continued her union work and by 1915 was the national organizer for the Amalgamated Union of Cooperative Employees (which later became the National Union of Distributive and Allied Workers). Her influence in union activities grew rapidly; she was a major figure in the many strikes of the cooperative employees.[4]

Miss Wilkinson was a woman of boundless energy and she committed herself totally to the causes she supported. As a result of her zeal, colleagues from time to time judged her as impetuous and imprudent—especially when she espoused Communist doctrine.[5] She joined the Communist Party when it founded in England in 1920 and supported several international organizations that were dominated by Communists. She was one of the first members of the British Bureau of the Red International of Labor Unions and an official leader of the Worker's International Relief.

Because Labor had not yet proscribed the Communists, Miss Wilkinson's activities did not alienate her from the party. She herself saw no conflict of loyalty in her Communist Party membership, because she also supported the Labor Party constitution. For their part, Labor Party leaders seem to have accepted her on her own terms. They elected her to serve on the Labor commission that conducted an inquiry into the conduct of the "Black and Tans" in Ireland during the Sinn Fein problems. Furthermore, in 1923 the Labor Party supported her candidacy for the Gorton South Ward Municipal seat on the Manchester City Council and her candidacy for Parliament to represent Ashton-under-Lyne. She won the municipal election but lost the Parliamentary contest.

Soon after assuming her seat on the Manchester City Council, Miss Wilkinson was appointed to the Education and Library Committees. When a majority of the Council voted to reduce the estimates of the Education Committee, the Labor Party organized a demonstration, and Miss Wilkinson was one of the key speakers. In her speech, she revealed that, although 7,000 to 8,000 Manchester children had been certified by examination as ready for secondary education, there was space in the schools for only 1,000. Additional secondary schools must be built, she declared. (This problem was widespread. Shortly after being appointed Minister of Education in 1945, by Clement Attlee, Miss Wilkinson reported that for the Cadiff High Schools, there were 2,267 children eligible for admittance but room for only 897.)[6]

In the year following her first Parliamentary campaign, Miss Wilkinson stood for Middlesborough East and captured the seat from a Liberal M.P. in a three-way fight. Her success was one of Labor's few gains in the General Election of 1924. It was attributed by some to the negative quality of the Conservative and Liberal campaigns—devoted "less to getting their own candidates in than keeping her out."[7] During this period, Miss Wilkinson was labeled by her opponents as a Communist—"the lady with the red hair and the red views."[8] Although this was an inaccurate representation—she had broken with the Communists because of their exclusiveness and their dictatorial policies—the image remained fixed in the public consciousness because the Communists supported her candidacy and because of her left-wing ideology. During her campaign she advocated public ownership of all large monopolies.

With her election in 1924 Miss Wilkinson entered a select group. She was one of four women M.P.s and the only woman not a Conservative. All four were under constant scrutiny from the press. Miss Wilkinson complained that the continual attention she received made it difficult for her to learn her job. Nevertheless, she seems to have enjoyed the spotlight: she filled the first twelve pages of her scrapbook for February 1925 to May 1926 with newspaper clippings that commented on her dress and hair. She made news because she was the first woman in the House of Commons to wear a colorful dress rather than the traditional black favored by Lady Astor and faithfully copied by other women M.P.s. She was the first to have her hair bobbed and even wore a monocle for a time. Several newspaper writers suggested that she was trying to "advertise herself."[9]

First Parliamentary Experience: 1924-1931

Ellen Wilkinson brought to her duties in Parliament a highly developed sense of social responsibility and a missionary's zeal. Her primary goals were to secure equal rights for all classes of women and to improve the lives of workers by helping to inaugurate a Socialist form of government. Her view of the world was distinctly Marxist; capitalists regarded workers as less than human, mere spokes in the wheels of industry. Their goal was to squeeze out high profits for their shareholders by keeping workers' wages at subsistence levels. Miss Wilkinson believed that, once workers were taught these "brutal facts," they would reject the capitalist system.[10] She was, she said, not against "the King, nor the House of Lords, but the small group who are interested in finance," that is, the bankers.[11] (Approximately 79% of the banking in England in the 1920s was controlled by five banks.) "Because of the national credit behind them," she stated, their profits were unconscionably high.[12] In her maiden speech in Parliament, Miss Wilkinson demanded equal franchise for women and criticized the Government's industrial and economic policies.

In the 1920s, women politicians were expected to devote themselves to issues affecting babies, health, and education.[13] Miss Wilkinson did, in fact, devote a great deal of effort to so-called "women's issues." Yet she did not want to be regarded only as a "woman's M.P.," for she devoted herself with equal concern to most of the pressing problems of her day.[14] As a dedicated foe of imperialism, she worked to protect the rights of people in the colonies. They should be educated by Britain to govern themselves, she believed, then granted independence. In actuality, she said, the colonies were being governed for "a very small white social interest."[15] When Government commissions visited the colonies on fact-finding tours, she noted, they seldom went beyond the enclaves of the ruling minority; they "wined and dined with the usual respectable people of the colony."[16] In the same anti-imperialist spirit, Miss Wilkinson opposed the Government's plan to send Britain troops to China in 1927 to protect the seven thousand "defenseless Britons in Shanghai."[17] She recommended that all Britons return to England, and that the British concessions should be surrendered.

During the same year Miss Wilkinson opposed the budget for the armed forces: the Government "had no money for social reforms, education or other national necessities but had voted 115 million for the armament of the country." She favored a general strike as the "only effective force" against militarism.[18]

Strong-minded and strong-willed, Miss Wilkinson's forthrightness often got her into trouble. "Patience is the worst vice that ever afflicted the human race," she said, a vice that she did not suffer in great quantity.[19] In 1927 she was nearly suspended from the service of the House, escaping official censure only by writing a letter of apology to Sir John Simon, Chairman of the Indian Commission, whom she had accused of acting "as the agent of the Indian Princes."[20] The experience hardly subdued her. A few years later she wrote in the Independent Labor Party newspaper that the Labor Secretary for Scotland, sixty-seven-year-old William Adamson, was "long past the work he had been given to do."[21] She got into trouble again in 1945 during a dock strike. In a talk about trade unionism with young people in Jarrow, she mentioned the possibility of bread rationing if the Canadian grain ships were not promptly unloaded so they could get to and from Canada before the rivers there froze. Because she was a member of the Government, this illustration of the possible effects of a strike was interpreted by the press and public as a Cabinet decision. The issue was raised in the House and she apologized, "I can merely say that in the future I shall be very careful in the illustrations that I use in making speeches."[22]

In 1924, Miss Wilkinson described women as "still the poor half of humanity,"[23] deprived of equal franchise, legal rights, and equal pay for equal work. As part of her campaign for legal equality for women, she proposed an Alien's bill that would amend the law that robbed a British woman of her citizenship when she married a foreigner, even if she never left Britain. No action was taken on her bill, however. The Government chose to wait until all the self-governing dominions agreed to the measure. In 1928, Miss Wilkinson asked the Prime Minister if he could "promise this reform within the lifetime of the present Parliament."[24] Because the Government wished to receive the report from the Committee of Experts created by the Imperial Conference of 1926 and then planned to call another Imperial Conference, the Prime Minister's answer was negative.

Miss Wilkinson was particularly sensitive to the need for more career opportunities for women. She recommended job training programs for women; supported the Municipal Corporation Act of 1882 Amendment Bill, which dealt with the hiring of women police; and protested to the Secretary of Commissions over the lack of women magistrates in the borough of Middlesborough.[25] She also sought to have the diplomatic service opened to women. During World War II, Miss Wilkinson pressed the Secretary of State to appoint a woman head of the Auxiliary Territorial Service at the War Office.[26] She also demanded a guarantee that no woman would be commissioned in this branch of service who was less than twenty-five, in an effort to avoid favored treatment for the socially prominent.[27] She also complained that women "belonging to the salary-earning classes, however intelligent and anxious to serve," were being overlooked when commissions in the Women's Auxiliary Territorial Service were awarded.[28] Commissions, she argued, should be given solely on merit.

Miss Wilkinson pressed for legislation that would ensure women better maternity care, because in the 1930s more women died in childbirth than men in the mines. (Lady Summerskill's campaign motto in the 1930s was "Better to be a miner than a mother.") She also supported Eleanor Rathbone's proposal for a family allowance plan, but wanted the money to be provided solely by the state rather than private employers. She proposed legislation that would make it illegal to specify "no children" in a contract for renting apartments.[29] She supported Margaret Bondfield's bill to supply clothing for children in areas where unemployment was rampant, and Susan Lawrence's bill to regulate the employment of children—the Children and Young Persons (Employment and Protection) Bill.

Although opportunities were beginning to open up for women, Miss Wilkinson noted that this did not include housewives who were busy looking after their homes. (She excluded wealthy M.P.s such as Lady Astor from the "housewife" category.) She hoped that more working women and especially more working-class married women would enter politics. Yet a woman with children should not enter Parliament, she said, until "adequate arrangements for the education of her children were made."[30] Unfortunately, only by "renouncing all home ties" could a woman be a Cabinet Minister.[31] Miss Wilkinson recognized that the question of marriage versus a career remained a personal decision. She herself never married, explaining that "there is such keen prejudice in England against the employment of married women that self-supporting women who have got along in a career are subconsciously swayed to accept it as their life work."[32]

Miss Wilkinson claimed that all the political parties in England discriminated against women. She attributed the fact, that only four women were elected to Parliament in 1924, compared to seven in 1923, to the parties' unfairness to women candidates.[33] Women were given the hardest seats to fight,[34] and the women's section of the Labor Party, which had done "magnificent work," was "too often starved of funds and speakers because the overwhelming importance of their work was not realized."[35]

As noted earlier, Miss Wilkinson did not limit her energies to the struggle for equal rights for women. She fought discrimination in any form. In 1925 she opposed the Government's plan to tax the "cheap silk used by the poor, which in some cases meant a tax of 160%, while the tax paid by 'my lady' worked out about 2%."[36] In 1927, she forced the Solicitor-General to admit that the Government did not recommend working-class men and women to serve as magistrates. He then agreed that if "the names of suitable working-class men and women were presented," they would be considered.[37] In 1931, she asked the Secretary of State for the Home Department to make it an offense under the licensing laws for proprietors to refuse to rent to nonwhites.

Miss Wilkinson also opposed discrimination closer to home. When the Socialist bachelors in the House of Commons held a singing party without inviting the single women, she protested: "In all things, I believe in sex equality, and if the Socialist members are going to sing, at least we should be asked to join in."[38] She had other complaints about Parliamentary customs. In 1927 there were eight women serving in Parliament. Yet these M.P.s were assigned the same accommodations that one—Lady Astor—had been given in 1918. Miss Wilkinson was one of the chief agitators for more space. She wrote a newspaper article describing the poor arrangements. For eight women there was one sitting room with three desks, two armchairs, two sofas, one clothes hook, and one small mirror. Their room was one-quarter of a mile from their one bath.[39] The women didn't get any sympathy from at least one of their male colleagues, the Reverend Hebert Dunnico, Labor M.P., who charged that Miss Wilkinson's complaints were a "piece of impertinence."[40] By the next year, however, the women had new rooms.[41]

In spite of, or perhaps because of, her outspoken manner, Miss Wilkinson was popular with her colleagues in the House of Commons. The bachelor members from all parties gave her an automatic gas stove for Christmas in 1928.[42] And she was the first woman M.P. to be called by nicknames: "our Ellen" by her party and "Miss Perky" by the House.

As with all M.P.s the demands on Miss Wilkinson's time were overwhelming. She attended committee meetings, investigated individual appeals, and kept abreast of pending legislation. She also handled all her own paperwork. The morning mail was "the most appalling task any M.P. has to face."[43] Despite these responsibilities, she found it necessary to supplement her salary by writing articles for several newspapers. She also kept up her union work—organizing meetings, writing pamphlets, and accepting speaking engagements.[44] Her work load was lightened considerably when Evelyn Preston, an American woman with a private income, volunteered to act as her secretary in 1926.

Throughout her parliamentary career, she was active in her party. She was elected to the Executive of the Trade Union Group of the Parliamentary Labor Party, a body that watched for any legislation aimed against labor unions. And as the chairman of the Standing Joint Committee of Working Women's Organizations, she presided over the National Conference of Labor Women held in Birmingham in the early summer of 1925. This was the first time the meeting had been chaired by a woman, although it was, in fact, a Labor women's conference. The Standing Committee was composed of representatives of the Labor Party, the Trade Union Congress, those trade unions with women members, and the Co-operative Movement.

As part of her efforts toward better working conditions, Miss Wilkinson introduced a Factories Bill and to extend its provisions to business offices. In 1927, she proposed the Offices Regulation Bill, which would regulate working conditions in offices as well as the employment of young people. Conditions in office buildings were unsafe and unsanitary: 122 out of every 1,000 workers died each year of pulmonary disease.[45] Under the new bill, employers would be compelled to paint their offices every seven years, to clean the windows every month, and to provide rest rooms for employees.

Along with her efforts to improve working conditions, Miss Wilkinson supported measures that would prevent the Government from taxing the working man. All the Labor M.P.s opposed the Government's proposed Widow's, Orphan's and Old Age Contributory Pensions Bill, because only the workers and their employers would put up the funds: "Thus the wealthy taxpayer contributed not a penny."[46] Most Labor members wanted a noncontributory pension plan instead. Miss Wilkinson pointed out that under the Government's plan the funds would not be allocated on a basis that reflected the greater needs of the widowed mother with dependent children as compared with the childless widow. Furthermore, unless the husband had been an insured contributor under the National Health Insurance Plan, the widow would get nothing. And if a wife with an invalid husband worked, she paid an insurance contribution but got no money when her husband died because a widow's pension "is drawn on her husband's contributions, not on her own."[47]

When the unrest in the mining industry culminated in the General Strike of 1926, Miss Wilkinson was often in the thick of battles on the floor of the House of Commons. She toured the country to address strike meetings, encouraging workers to realize that their most powerful weapons were "their vote, their trade unions, and their cooperative societies."[48] She was convinced that the miners' only real hope for redress of grievances was nationalization of the mining industry. In August of 1926 she went to America with Ben Tillett as a delegate appointed by the Trade Union Congress to raise money for the strikers. They hoped to raise 250,000 pounds but found that an unofficial group had already canvassed America. The identity of this unofficial group was vague and very little of the money raised by them ever reached the strikers.[49]

By 1930 the Labor Government was struggling with the problem of unemployment. Speaking again in the United States, Miss Wilkinson told an audience that the British Government had supplied money to the local authorities and now it was up to these authorities to "produce schemes" to solve the unemployment problem.[50] By July of 1930 unemployment in Miss Wilkinson's constituency had risen to 50%. She accused the Middlesborough authorities of the "blacklegging of trade unions" by using men who were on relief for municipal jobs that ought to be done by ordinary paid labor at "trade union rate of wages."[51] She believed that one solution to help the problem of unemployment would be to begin trade with Russia. Because the Labor Party was powerless in this matter, she proposed that the president of the Board of Trade instigate such a policy.

As Labor struggled with the problem of government in 1930, Miss Wilkinson condemned members of the British press who blamed her party for the country's problems. In fact, she said, MacDonald's government was doing "ambulance work, cleaning up the mess left by their predecessors."[52] (Ramsay MacDonald was Prime Minister of the Labor Government that was elected in 1929.) Miss Wilkinson urged her party to ignore the newspapers' "propaganda." To leave things as they were or only to "tidy them up," as the press advocated, would mean that "we are only Liberals."[53] After Labor lost the General Election in 1931, Miss Wilkinson visited the editor of the *Daily Express*. Their conversation included the following exchange:

> Miss Wilkinson: *"I congratulate you!"*
> Editor: *"On what?"*
> Miss Wilkinson: *"On the most perfect and unscrupulous political campaign in history."*[54]

Years Out of Parliament: 1931-1935

When the Labor Party was rejected by the voters in 1931, all four women M.P.s then serving in the House of Commons were defeated. No new Labor women members were elected. Miss Wilkinson blamed Labor's loss on the conservatism and timidity of Labor Party members, as well as the attacks of the press.[55] Her party, she said, had adopted the philosophy that "the old system worked, so we'll patch it up again."[56] She believed that the Labor movement should have introduced Socialism in order to help the working class. The major problem, she said, was "overproduction, coupled with the fact that most of the people could not afford to buy back the goods produced."[57] The party leaders, in her opinion, made a major mistake in using the term "reorganization" instead of "nationalization." They should have stated boldly that they favored "replacement of private Capitalism by nationally-owned resources."[58]

After leaving Parliament Miss Wilkinson made the most of her freedom to travel. She visited India, Russia, France, Germany, Italy, and the United States. During her visits to the United States she was well received, despite her criticisms of the country. She disclaimed any unity of viewpoint between England and the United States simply because

we "happen to speak the same language."[59] Furthermore, she had a
very low opinion of the American politician: he had gone into politics,
she said, "either because he was not one of the bright boys and could
not make a good businessman, or because he had a 'racket' or was going
into 'graft' reasons."[60]

Miss Wilkinson made her first visit to Russia in 1931. She became
convinced that Russia was a better place than the United States and
that all the stories of atrocities were inventions of the press. She hoped
that the British people would take a warmer attitude toward Russia,
and, in particular, that the Labor Party would end its feud with that
country.

In 1932, Miss Wilkinson made her first trip to India. She was leader
of a fact-finding group that also included Monica Whately, Leonard W.
Matters, and J. K. Krishna Menon. The group had been appointed by
the India League and spent three months in India. Their visit received
quite a bit of publicity in England. Sir Samuel Hoare, Secretary for
India, criticized the group on the floor of the House of Commons:

> According to detailed reports from practically every district they visited,
> they did not seem anxious to avail themselves of official offers of help,
> and were not disposed to credit accurate information when it was sup-
> plied to them. The party as a whole chose throughout to take its impres-
> sions from the Congress workers, who are known to have received careful
> instructions from their headquarters as to staging for their benefit Congress
> demonstrations which would involve clashes with police and so on.[61]

Upon her return to England, Miss Wilkinson gave numerous speeches.
She had, she said, seen India as the Indians see it.[62] British soldiers were
being used by Bombay mill owners to maintain control of the workers.
The very term used in England—"holding" India—was descriptive of the
attitude of the "vested interest."[63] As a fervent supporter of Mahatma
Gandhi, who had made the "Indians get on their feet and realize that
when they want their country they can have it," she denounced the
British efforts to suppress his leadership.[64]

During this same period, Miss Wilkinson traveled to Spain as a
member of a commission sent by the Labor Party to evaluate the rebel-
lion in Asturias. The commission was instructed to investigate the "al-
leged cruel repression of Spanish Socialists and Communists during the
revolt in October."[65] The hostility of the crowds cut short the investi-
gation, but Spain remained a focus of her interest.[66] She was highly
critical of the British Government's action during the Spanish Civil
War, and, in particular, of their failure to sell arms to Spain so that it
might "maintain order in its own country."[67] While on a visit to Spain
in 1939, she attended a reception in Madrid, where she was introduced
to a Consular official whom she believed to be pro-Franco. She "drew"

herself up to her full height (which was not great) and, looking at him with blazing eyes, repeated his name twice. She then made a deep curtsey and turned away. "It was very impressive. . . ."[68]

It was the Fascist activity in Spain that first caused Miss Wilkinson to modify her opposition to military spending. Although she still believed that war was a "capitalist endeavor," she could not allow Britain to remain defenseless before the onslaught of German militarism: "The Fascist menace has to be considered today."[69] The League of Nations offered little hope for peace, she stated, while "every month there is a fresh humiliation of this Government before the Fascists."[70] She strongly opposed appeasement. Britain had already gone too far in giving up Spain and Czechoslovakia.[71] Her own flat was the center of activity for the Committee for the Victims of German Fascism.[72] In 1934, as she tried to arouse the public, she was predicting that the "next war would be fought entirely in the air," and that the "Jews and Socialists in Germany are going to get it in the neck."[73]

Return to Parliament: 1935-1947

Miss Wilkinson was ready for political action when a General Election was called in 1935. She was put forward by the Labor Party as the proposed candidate for the industrial town of Jarrow, but her candidacy met with strong local resistance. The miners of the area wanted a man to represent them, because "politics have become largely economic, and an intricate fiscal business."[74] George Harvey, a checkweighman in the mines, was the miners' favorite, but the management Committee selected Miss Wilkinson. As a result, M. J. Coutts, the party agent for many years, resigned. However, Miss Wilkinson's devotion to her constituency soon healed the local party rift.

Miss Wilkinson's Parliamentary activities from 1935 to the beginning of World War II were similar to her entire experiences in the House of Commons. The major issue remained unemployment. Her own constituency of Jarrow was one of the most depressed areas in the country. Conditions there gained national attention in 1936 during the famous Jarrow March. This six-day march of two hundred unemployed men, some of whom had been without work for fifteen years, covered three hundred miles. It terminated in London, where a petition requesting Government help in supplying work for the borough was presented at the Bar of the House of Commons by Ellen Wilkinson herself.

Despite the disapproval of the Labor Party, Miss Wilkinson helped to organize and support the Jarrow March, as well as participating in it personally. At the annual Labor Party Conference in Edinburgh, which took place during the March, she pleaded for help for the unemployed.

When a proposal for another report on the situation was advanced, she expressed her anger: Had there not already been enough reports? Lucy Middleton, wife of the Labor Party Secretary, and also a prospective candidate for Parliament, did not support Ellen's views: It was "better to send out good people to spread the word, not hungry men on marches."[75] The Conference did resolve that the employment fund surpluses of the Party should be given to the unemployed, with an increase in the rate of benefit. Nevertheless, the actions of the Conference infuriated the people of Jarrow. They resented being called "ill-clad, and underfed," and protested the treatment accorded Miss Wilkinson.[76]

The town of Jarrow was united in support of the March. It was sanctioned by the Town Council. The men were accompanied on the first part of their trip by the Mayor of Jarrow, by Ellen Wilkinson, and by many members of the Town Council.[77] Although the March was well publicized, it was a surprisingly uneventful affair. There was "no trace of party spirit or political propaganda."[78] There were only a few scattered incidents. In one case a young man "who wished to wave a banner was stopped because he was a Communist," and a town missioner was only allowed to give the marchers a copy of the Gospel of St. John on the condition that it contained "no sectarian matters."[79]

The Government viewed the Jarrow March with suspicion. A statement was issued that "in the opinion of His Majesty's Government such marchers can do no good to the causes for which they are represented to be undertaken and are altogether undesirable."[80] It was agreed among the Conservatives that Miss Wilkinson would be received by the Prime Minister or by cabinet ministers, but not as a leader of the deputation from the marchers. She countered by ignoring the leadership; the marchers were there to present a petition not to the Government but to Parliament, she said. She noted that "when a deputation arrives in cars there never seems to be any difficult whatever in their being received."[81] The Government had the last word, however: they cut the unemployment benefits of many of the marchers for two weeks because they had been unavailable for work.[82]

By 1939, the situation was still so bad that a figure of 3.5 million unemployed was being predicted. Miss Wilkinson believed that the only solution was the nationalization of finance, land, transport, coal, and power. The economic system of the capitalistic world had only been kept going "at all because of armament orders and war schemes."[83]

The unemployment issue was pushed into the background as the threat of war moved closer to Britain. Acting on the advice of the national executive committee of the Labor Party, Clement Attlee, leader of the party, and Arthur Greenwood, his deputy, refused to serve in a National Government headed by Neville Chamberlain. As the country grew uneasy about Chamberlain's leadership and as Labor withdrew its support, he was persuaded to resign. Winston Churchill was selected to lead the Coalition Government. Miss Wilkinson described the war years as an "election truce" not a "political truce."[84] However, her dedicated work within the coalition government led some of Britain's leftists to call her "a hireling of the capitalist."

Churchill appointed Miss Wilkinson to the post of Parliamentary Secretary to the Ministry of Pensions. This Ministry not only awarded pensions[85] but also worked on solutions to problems concerning workmen's compensation, e.g., who pays workers injured during the air raid?[86] As a member of the Government, she threw herself into her new job with her usual enthusiasm. She felt Britain must keep its production steady and maintain as normal a life as possible during the war. She visited several camps set up for children removed from the coastal areas by the government and urged the children to remain in these camps. Their job during the war, she said, was to remain safe: "You are the people who must run England in the future."[87]

After she had served only a few months at the Ministry of Pensions, Herbert Morrison requested Miss Wilkinson's service as one of two Parliamentary Secretaries assigned to the Ministry of Home Security. (She shared this appointment with William Mabane for two years. When he left the Ministry in 1942, she absorbed his responsibility for "wages, welfare, laborers and accommodations.")[88] Her first assignment in the Ministry was the regulation of air raid shelters. First, she visited scattered shelters to make a firsthand evaluation. She found that many were completely unorganized, with no provision for the ill and invalid; one East End shelter held 14,000 people.[89] Others needed to be replaced because "contractors fell into temptation when the cement regulations were relaxed."[90]

Herbert Morrison also selected Miss Wilkinson to be Britain's first fire-watcher chief, in an attempt to bring all fire-fighting resources under a central government control.[91] Previously, each town had had its own fire-prevention scheme, but now all towns were short of volunteers. By July of 1942, "fire had become the main problem of civil defense."[92] Because water mains often failed during raids, Miss Wilkinson proposed a compulsory scheme whereby all households would be required to store four gallons of water. She also advocated the compulsory training of all fire-watchers "in the characteristics of fire bombs, use of appliances and operational use of fireguard parties."[93] The most pressing problem confronting her, however, was the lack of women volunteers for fire-watching. She complained that there "were a number of younger women in the country, particularly those from well-to-do families, who have deliberately neglected to register under the National Registration Act."[94] A threat of conscription brought a tremendous public outcry. Although she held a press conference to explain her position, she could answer only a fraction of the written criticisms that surged into the Ministry. Women fire-watchers, she said, would be used "in only one of two places, either in their own streets or in places where they worked."[95] Nevertheless, her own union, the National Union of Distributive and Allied Workers, "denounced her for making women fire-watch."[96]

Miss Wilkinson spent her days at her desk and her evenings driving around London "encouraging and inspiring sweating civilian defenders."[97] She drove her own car rather than use the Ministerial chauffeur. She did not want to expose a married man with children to such a risk. Although the war monopolized the major portion of her attention, her interest in social and economic problems did not lessen. She succeeded in getting a private members' bill, the Hire Purchase Act of 1938, through Parliament. This was designed to protect the consumer who bought an article on credit and then found that he or she could not keep up the payments. With high unemployment, this was a frequent occurrence. Prior to passage of the bill, a company could legally repossess the article with no credit given for payments made even if 95% of the original purchase price had been paid. Miss Wilkinson recommended that if 25% of the purchase price had been paid before the article was repossessed, one-half of the amount already paid had to be refunded. The bill was fought by hire traders but was passed by Parliament without a dissenting voice.[98]

As soon as World War II ended, the parties began preparing for the General Election of 1945. Miss Wilkinson was both Chairman of the National Executive, having succeeded to the chair by seniority and a Member of the Campaign Committee. She was in the presidential chair of the Labor Party conference held at Blackpool in the spring of 1945, and "by common consent had been the most competent."[99] She, too, reentered the political arena, still distrusting both the press and big business, who "were the enemies of the Labor Party in this fight."[100]

The election conditions were chaotic. Because no Parliamentary register had been prepared since 1939, civilian identity cards were used. Servicemen's votes had to be flown back to England for counting. Although the voting took place on July 5, it was not until July 26 that the results were announced. Labor had won a clear victory with an overall majority of 152. Furthermore, twenty-four women had been elected: twenty-one Labor, one Conservative, one Liberal, and one Independent.

Miss Wilkinson's years of political experience and party work were rewarded when Prime Minister Clement Attlee appointed her Minister of Education. This made her the second woman to hold a cabinet post. (Margaret Bondfield had been the first.) Attlee recalled that Miss Wilkinson "looked a little surprised" when he selected her for this position.[101] She had been part of a group backing Herbert Morrison to replace Attlee as leader of the Labor Party; no doubt "she had not expected such magnanimity."[102] Her actions on Morrison's behalf had been received with indignation by members of the National Executive, of which she was a member representing the Women's Section.[103] There was a proposal for condemnation of her, but opinion was divided, even though she was not popular with most of the men at the best of times.[104] Attlee wrote that he appointed her because she had done a good job as a junior minister, because she was "an enthusiast for education," and because some women should be appointed to such jobs as education or National Insurance.[105]

Ellen Wilkinson in her role as Minister of Education faced overwhelming problems, problems that were magnified by wartime shortages. There were not enough school buildings or materials to construct new ones. There was a shortage of paper, books, and printing supplies. The paper quota for school printing in 1946 was only seventy percent of the 1939 figure. There were not enough teachers or training colleges to supply more. Special training schools for teachers were created, but it was difficult to take manpower out of the existing work force, because there was already a shortage.

The Government was on record as favoring the raising of the school-leaving age to fifteen by April 1, 1946. This was a goal dear to Miss Wilkinson's heart. Raising the age to fifteen, however, meant that an additional 370,000 people would be withdrawn from the work force. Furthermore, an increase in students called for an additional increase in teaching staff. In Wales alone, this increase would create a need for 850 more teachers.

In her position as Minister of Education, Miss Wilkinson sought to make education available to all children solely on the basis of merit. Options were available to her that had not been available to her predecessors, because the Education Act of 1944 gave the Ministry new powers. Previously, the Ministry could supply money and determine the number of teachers in each area, but local authorities made all policy decisions in conjunction with teachers. After 1944 the Minister could overrule local authorities on educational matters, and each area was ordered to submit a developmental plan for approval. Nevertheless, Miss Wilkinson was helpless to intervene in the hiring practice of the local authorities, even when cases of sex discrimination were revealed.[106]

The purpose of the Education Act was to make the English educational system uniform. There were to be three types of secondary school: the grammar schools for college preparation, the technical schools for students with manual aptitudes, and the modern schools for the "average" students, who formed the bulk of the school-age population. This plan was criticized by many as "promulgating a wrong social philosophy," but Miss Wilkinson favored it because students' placements were determined solely on the basis of merit.[107]

The two big questions in the minds of educators when Miss Wilkinson took her position were: Can school-leaving age be raised to fifteen by 1946 or 1947, and will local authorities produce their Developmental Schemes? One of her last public acts before her sudden death was to announce that the school-leaving age would be raised, as planned, on April 1, 1947.

Miss Wilkinson was never physically strong, but she seldom allowed her frequent illnesses to keep her from fulfilling her political obligations. Her doctors were continually in despair at her refusal to take better care of herself. She was also accident-prone and suffered several falls both at home and in Parliament. In addition, she was involved in several automobile accidents. Nevertheless, her death from an overdose of drugs on February 6, 1947, was totally unexpected. She was rushed to St. Mary's Hospital in Paddington after being found unconscious in her apartment. Suffering from asthma and bronchitis, she had been using both anti-asthmatic medication and sleeping tablets. However, there was "no shred of evidence that the overdose was taken deliberately."[108]

Miss Wilkinson was buried in Penn Street, Buckinghamshire. This was the village, thirty miles from London, where she had spent her weekends in a small cottage. She particularly loved the garden, where she had been able to unwind on weekends. A simple stone engraved "1891 E. W. 1947" marks her grave.[109] Her entire estate of 7,253 pounds was left to her sister Anne, who had been her constant companion.

❁   ❁   ❁

In addition to her political life, Miss Wilkinson had had some success as an author. Her first book, the novel *Clash*, was published in 1929. The background of the novel was the General Strike of 1926. It portrayed "all the strains of modern life, the clash of classes," and it was also a vindication of the right of women to continue their careers after marriage.[110] Although the book was well received by the critics and the public, the reaction from the trade unions was negative. It was rumored that they didn't like the picture she had presented of the labor movement.[111]

In 1930 she wrote a series of characterizations of selected members of Parliament and compiled them into a book entitled *Peeps at Politicians*. In 1932, her mystery, the *Division Bell Mystery*, was given favorable reviews. In it the House of Commons was a setting for a murder.

Miss Wilkinson's last book, The *Town That Was Murdered*, was written in 1939 and is her best-known. Miss Wilkinson used the town of Jarrow, "the classic town of unemployment in England," as an example of the evils inherent in the capitalist system.[112] The fate suffered by Jarrow demonstrated that if industry is organized for private profit, successful planning is impossible and the economy of the nation is restricted.

In the first section of the book, Miss Wilkinson traced the industrial history of Jarrow from the early nineteenth century, when it was an expanding coal mining town, to mid-nineteenth century, when coal production declined. The owners of the mines made personal fortunes as the rich veins were worked by men lured from their subsistence farm life to the town by relatively high wages. As the work force grew, the employers kept wages at a minimum, because labor costs were the highest item in coal production. Low wages meant higher profits. This was the reason that coal mining was "the classic battleground of the class struggle."[113] As the profitability of the mines declined, the employers made even more demands upon the workers in an effort to maintain their own profits. The mine owners could never agree to work together on any activity except "against the men."[114]

In the early years, the workers were an illiterate unorganized group opposed by the entire establishment, including the "manager who got them to sign the bond, administered it as a magistrate and could send them to prison for 'crimes' that he listed."[115] If they tried to strike, the police and army were called out against them with the blessing of both the middle and upper classes, as well as the church. From this isolated position, the workers' "sense of solidarity in the class struggle grew."[116] Miss Wilkinson disputed the popular theory that local capitalists were more interested in the welfare of their workers than London investors. She contended that all capitalists were interested only in profits.

In the second industrial development of Jarrow, the shipbuilding industry grew as the mines declined. Because many more workers were needed, the town grew tremendously. This growth led to overcrowded conditions and disease. She described this period as a time when "a whole working-class was exploited to the limit, its strength sucked by long hours, and by wages which kept most workers at the level of deadly malnutrition."[117] Yet when the shipyard was short of work, the men were laid off and their lives were even more desperate.

The decline in trade in the 1890s led to deeper suffering among the workers. Organization of the workers began to make headway during this period. As union activity increased, workers turned to politics. A labor candidate was entered in the General Election of 1892, although he was defeated.

The advent of World War I brought work and wage increases. But the decline of the shipyard shortly after the war was "an object lesson in the mismanagement of a great national asset of high technical efficiency, by men whose whole interest lay in the amount of profit that could be squeezed out rapidly with little regard to national interest . . . or of those whose livelihood and interest depended on it."[118] As prosperity declined after the war, the employers "prepared to face the crises by an attack on wage rates."[119]

Sir James Lithgow organized National Shipbuilding Security, Ltd., to concentrate production, minimize overhead, and make possible a suitable increase in prices. This group bought struggling shipyards, sold the machinery for scrap, and refused to release the site for future shipyards for a term of forty years. When they took over in Jarrow, virtually everyone in the town was jobless by 1933.

Efforts were made to use the site for the construction of an integrated steel plant, but the steel cartel prevented this, fearing that a modern plant would produce steel at a lower cost and that the older plants would not be able to compete. They would allow the industry to be modernized only if they could maintain control sufficient to prevent their products being undersold. This was a "vivid illustration of the obstacles put in the way of technical progress by modern monopoly capitalism when it can secure a complacent government to provide the necessary legislative conditions for a closed market at the expense of the taxpayers."[120] Jarrow did eventually get a steel mill, but it was not the large integrated one originally proposed.

On the whole, the reviews of Miss Wilkinson's book were very good, with note taken, however, that the Jarrow story was told from a "Socialist viewpoint."[121]

Conclusion

Ellen Wilkinson is a typical "Pioneer" Labor Party Member of Parliament. She was part of a working-class family, won scholarships and educational and political opportunities through her own ability, and then used her political power to help those who were discriminated against because of sex, class, creed, or color. Her compassion embraced all people and all classes.

Miss Wilkinson respected ability regardless of party. An admirer of Winston Churchill, she was the first to stand and applaud his entrance into the House after World War II ended. But she knew class differences to be an insurmountable barrier in Parliament, as elsewhere. Describing a dispute betwen two Labor Party mmbers, George Buchanan and Lady Cynthia Mosley, she wrote: "They were members of the same political party, avowing the same social ideals, but the great barrier was between them as surely and as deeply as though the Marquis Curzon's daughter had stayed with her own class and the party of her ancestors."[122]

As a woman M.P., Miss Wilkinson often felt like an outsider. Once she was asked if there were room for more women like herself in the House of Commons. She responded, "If you ask the House of Commons, they will say no."[123] Yet after her death, a memorial service was held in Parliament and leaders from all parties paid their last respects to "Miss Perky."

3
Eleanor Florence Rathbone

Eleanor Florence Rathbone was elected to Parliament as an Independent in the General Election of 1929 to represent the Combined English Universities (Manchester, Birmingham, Leeds, Sheffield, Durham, Bristol, and Reading). She served this constituency until her death in January 1946.[1] Throughout her career, her name was linked with the cause of women's rights, as an active suffragist, an originator of the Family Allowance Plan, and an advocate for increased governmental responsibility for the rights of women throughout the Empire—India, Africa, and the Middle East.

Miss Rathbone's family, the Rathbones of Liverpool, had begun in the early eighteenth century an unbroken tradition of involvement in social and political causes. The first William Rathbone lived in the village of Gawsworth in the country of Cheshire. His descendants, five more William Rathbones including Miss Rathbone's father, lived in Liverpool, building a flourishing shipbuilding business and establishing reputations for integrity and public service.

> Given a knowledge of the conflicts which at various points have agitated Liverpool, one can deduce with accurate precision what the contemporary William Rathbone will be doing: opposing the slave trade, constructing a health service, abolishing the Poor Law, founding a university.[2]

The wives of the successive William Rathbones had contributed their individual energies to the family penchant for social causes, and the women of the family were an acknowledged source of its strength.

With this background, it was not surprising that Eleanor Rathbone chose to begin her career, after studies in philosophy at Somerville College at Oxford, as a social worker in Liverpool. Her grasp of the problems of poverty, and especially of the injustices suffered by women of the lowest economic strata, led her inevitably into local politics. She became the first woman to serve on the Liverpool City Council. But it was the concern for women of another country—the British colony of India, as described by Katharine Mayo in *Mother India*—that provided the catalyst for Miss Rathbone's first successful bid for Parliament.

33

As an Independent M.P., Miss Rathbone was not subject to party disciplines. She did not hesitate to criticize policies advocated by the parties: the Conservative Government's appeasement of Nazi Germany and the Labor Party's pacifism in the 1930s, for example. Although her political independence was the natural consequence of her personal way of life, it exacted penalties. She did not have a party to unite behind her proposals, and she did not have the research facilities available to party members. Despite her solitary position, however, she was not easily overlooked by her colleagues in Parliament. What they were always keenly aware of was her selfless, single-minded, sometimes formidable determination. Harold Nicholson, writing for the *Spectator* after her death, described her effect on her fellow M.P.s:

> Benign and yet menacing, she would stalk through the lobby, one arm weighed with the heavy satchel which contained the papers on family allowances, another arm dragging an even heavier satchel in which were stored the more recent papers about refugees and displaced persons; recalcitrant Ministers would quail before the fire of her magnificent eyes. . . . yet although in attack she was as undeviating, as relentless and as pertinacious as a flying bomb, in the moment of victory she was amazingly conciliatory. While the battle was on, she displayed all the passion of the fanatic; when the enemy yielded, she advanced towards him bearing the olive branch of compromise.[3]

Even today her reputation for independence is very much alive in England. When a taxi driver in London learned that I was studying British political history, his comment was: "I wish we still had the University seat. Members like Miss Rathbone looked after their country rather than their parties."

❋   ❋   ❋

Eleanor Rathbone was born in London in 1892, the only member of the Rathbone family to be born outside of Liverpool. Her father, William Rathbone VI, was a Gladstonian Liberal who had been elected to Parliament in 1868. Thus, the family spent at least half of every year in London. It was while Parliament was in session that Eleanor was born, the ninth of ten children.[4]

Like her brothers and sisters, Eleanor Rathbone was rooted in Liverpool. Like them, too, she received her early education from a series of undistinguished tutors and governesses and for a brief period attended a private school in London. Although she could not enter Liverpool University, which her family had helped to found, because of her sex, she was able to attend Somerville College at Oxford. Women at Oxford could then attend lectures, work with tutors, and take examinations, but were not considered full members of the University. Miss Rathbone's field was philosophy and among her friends she was known as "The Philosopher," much as we in this country might call someone "the absent-minded professor." She was noted for her devotion to her studies and her indifference to the ordinary details of daily life. These Oxford friends, all women, constituted a group known to themselves as the A.P.s, the "Associated Prigs." They met informally at frequent intervals to discuss Socialism, factory legislation, the Poor Law, and other political and philosophical topics. During these years and throughout her life, Miss Rathbone's only close personal attachments, outside her family, were with women. In a letter to one of these Oxford friends a few years after returning to Liverpool she described how her life had changed:

> When one is young and a newcomer in the world, one looks at it all in a detached way, wondering why the inhabitants take themselves and their trivial affairs so seriously, and finding one's chief interests outside it. But by degrees one warms to one's fellow mortals, and the danger becomes that one should lose the power of detaching oneself to the extent necessary for serving it most effectively. Of course, this does mean that one almost inevitably has one's sense of proportion spoiled—and in a world where everyone was as well off as oneself, the utilitarian spirit might be a thing to fight against. But in *such* a world with all its wrong shouting in one's ears and every miserable face claiming kinship, how can one be *sorry* that it is no longer easy to shut one's ears and revel in thought for thought's sake.[5]

Miss Rathbone began a career as a social worker in 1897, serving as a Visitor for the Liverpool Central Relief Society. At the same time, and until his death in 1902, she was her father's assistant and companion as he devoted himself to charitable works in Liverpool. With an intense belief in the individual's ability to bring about change, William Rathbone's credo was severe and straightforward: "Whatever ought to be done, can be done."[6] Despite her attachment to her father, Miss Rathbone was always her own woman, committing herself to projects and causes beyond those associated with her family. An articulate feminist since her years at Oxford, her ideology was strengthened by her social work experience. "The reason that the claim of widows for different treatment (under the Poor Law) has been so long unrecognized is clearly not far to seek," she wrote in a pamphlet entitled *The Conditions of Widows under the Poor Law in Liverpool;* "All widows are women, and none of them therefore are Parliamentary voters."[7]

In her first years as a social worker, Miss Rathbone was, in the words of one biographer, "a Prig—no longer Associated." She was highly critical of other Visitors—lower middle-class people, very willing and interested, but not highly educated and quite untrained. She saw her job in those early days as a matter of teaching the poor to be thrifty, goading them if necessary by fear of the workhouse into more frugal habits. As her experience deepened, she realized that the pattern of underemployment for casual laborers caused the pervasive impoverishment that the Visitors were powerless to cure. On the basis of a study of employment on the Liverpool docks, she published *How the Casual Labourer Lives* in 1909. In it she proposed a system of clearinghouses for workers that was eventually adopted by the docks.

She was already well known as a member of the respected Rathbone family, and by 1909 her twelve years of work among the poor of Liverpool had "attracted to her side a very fine army of fellow workers capable of conducting a social survey, building up an organization, or winning an election. . . ."[8] She was elected to represent the Granby Ward as the first woman member of the Liverpool Council, a position she held until 1935.

During the next several years her legislative interests centered around municipal housing. At the same time she was active on the Executive Committee of the National Union of Women's Suffrage Societies (N.U.-W.S.S.), a position that involved her in her first political battle within feminist ranks. The issue was whether the organization should continue to support all Labor party candidates for Parliament, the official Labor position on women's suffrage being in the affirmative. When she failed in her attempt to reverse the policy espoused by Millicent Garrett Fawcett and other N.U.W.S.S. leaders, in favor of independent judgment of individual candidates, Miss Rathbone resigned. The year was 1914. A few months later the feminists turned from ideology to the common war effort, and, like many of her colleagues in the movement, Eleanor Rathbone entered a new stage of political life.

In Liverpool, as in towns and cities throughout Britain, a branch of the Soldiers' and Sailors' Families Association was given the task of finding funds to support the working-class families of newly conscripted servicemen. Once the initial crises were surmounted, she worked on a day-to-day basis with women who had to provide for their children on meager government allowances until their men returned. What differentiated these sparse allotments from the regular pay of husbands and fathers was that they were determined by the size of the family rather than the nature of the father's job. In addition, these allowances were paid directly to the mothers, reflecting the reality of family care arrangements. As a result of her wartime experiences, Miss Rathbone published an article in the *Economic Journal* of March 1917 calling for a permanent program of family allowances. In October of that year she convened a group of seven people who formed the Family Endowment Committee. The other members were Kathleen Courtney, Mary Stocks, Maude Royden, H. N. Brailsford, and Mr. and Mrs. Emile Burns. In 1918, the group went out of existence, having published a pamphlet entitled *Equal*

Pay and the Family: A Proposal for the National Endowment of Mother-hood.

Many of the members of the Family Endowment Committee were members of N.U.W.S.S. All were active in the battle for enfranchisement that culminated in the Representation of the People Act of 1918. Miss Rathbone played an important part in the framing of the bill. She is credited with the inclusion of local as well as national elections in the provisions that granted suffrage to all women over thirty who were single freeholders or wives of freeholders. As in many political battles to follow, she had the vision to seize the opportunity to gain as much as possible for women, despite the fear of many feminists that both local and national suffrage might be too much for the men in Parliament to swallow at one time.

First Stand for Parliament, 1922

Miss Rathbone made her first bid for Parliament in the General Election of 1922. She chose to stand as an Independent for the East Toxteth Division of Liverpool "because I want to let my vote follow my conviction rather than a party whip,"[9] and likened her candidacy to David's contest with Goliath. It did seem presumptuous to many voters that she dared to stand as an Independent candidate when women did not have the right to vote. Her opponents asked: "Isn't it rather ridiculous for a man to vote for a woman representative?" "Not more ridiculous" she replied, "than it is for a woman to canvass for a man."[10] One of her campaign slogans was "Vote for the best man, this time a woman."

Miss Rathbone's experience in local government, in the suffragist movement, and in social work had given her invaluable exposure and political experience. Furthermore, she was backed by both the Liverpool Women's Citizen Association, "the best organized in the country," and the Liberal Party.[11] The cornerstones of her campaign platforms were "peace" and "stability." She advocated strengthening the League of Nations and a reduction in all nations' armaments. These reductions, she claimed, would lower taxes at home, causing prices to fall and reviving trade. If a Free Trade policy were also followed, the unemployment problem would be alleviated. The unemployed could be further assisted through the expansion of public works. She also proposed pensions for widows with children, improved secondary education, and the demolition of slums.[12]

The most damaging charge brought against Miss Rathbone by her opponents was that she was a Socialist. One of the city councillors,

M. J. Albert Thompson, "asserted that 90 percent of the votes given by Miss Rathbone in the Council were on Socialistic questions."[13] At one meeting she was asked if it were true "that you are in favor of domestic servants receiving a minimum of £1 a week with fifteen hours off?"[14] Miss Rathbone attempted to defuse these charges: "I am not a Socialist in the ordinary sense of the term," she stated.[15] She wanted, she said, to improve social conditions but not to nationalize private property.

Her opponents attacked her plan for a family allowance in an anonymous pamphlet distributed a few days before the election. She tried to counter this by explaining in newspaper articles that she intended this plan to be put into action through cooperative efforts of employers and employees rather than through legislation: individual wages would be determined by labor negotiations. Additionally, these wages would be supplemented by allowances based on the number of dependent children in a family. Money for these allowances would come from a pool created by the contributions of employers, based on the total number of employees. (Thus the employers would have no incentive to hire only unmarried men.)[16] Miss Rathbone was soundly defeated by the Conservative candidate, J. S. Rankin.

During this period, London had become Miss Rathbone's headquarters, even though she was still City Councillor for Liverpool. In London, she had her good friend, Elizabeth Macadam, for companionship, and her work as president of the National Union of Society for Equal Citizenship. She had also been steadily at work trying to gain acceptance for her Family Endowment Plan. Miss Rathbone believed the payment of a living wage was compulsory if Britain was to "remain a Godly nation" and nationally strong. In an effort to present a coherent view of her proposals, she wrote *The Disinherited Family* in 1924. She began her book with an examination of the successful family endowment efforts made by other nations, in order to show that the proposal was feasible. She contended that in Britain the entire family had traditionally been forced to work. After the Industrial Revolution, Parliament passed protective legislation to limit the work of children and women. This humanitarian effort resulted in making the family head the sole provider. The family head was forced to earn enough to support the entire family. Yet the wage earner generally reached his maximum salary as a young, single man. As his family increased, his wages remained stationary. Miss Rathbone proposed a "claim for horizontal redistribution, i.e. for the family as against the individual."[17]

Society should be held responsible for the creation of an economic structure for "some kind of direct provision for the financial cost of rearing children instead of leaving it to be met through the ordinary wage system."[18] The pool system appeared to be the most feasible means of achieving this end. The families would be provided for "out of a pool fed by contributions from the product of industry."[19] This pool could be either an occupational pool or a state endowment from which money would be taken to give workers an additional proportion of their income. The money would be paid to the mother, with a fixed amount for each child. This amount would be based on a proportion of the stabilized cost of living for two people. This was essentially the same system that Miss Rathbone had been supporting since 1909 and described during her campaign for the Liverpool City Council.

In an effort to gather support for her plan, Miss Rathbone spoke before Parliamentary groups, contacted influential people, and tried to persuade members of Equal Citizenship (the successor of N.U.W.S.S.) to make the plan a plank in their platform. The strongest opposition came from the Conservative and Liberal parties. Economists were also doubtful for they questioned the results of the "additional charges on industry or the tax-payer."[20]

In general, the fears were that such a scheme would lead to over-population as well as the loss of parental responsibility and all efforts at thrift. But there was also the "Turk Theory," so named by Miss Rathbone, which referred to the "refusal of men with no children to accept less wages than others."[21]

Individual members of the Labor Party were more sympathetic to Miss Rathbone's plan. The Independent Labor Party gave its official support at its annual conference in 1926. The Labor Party, however, feared that adoption of such a plan "might complicate and possibly bedevil the traditional conception of a standard wage, the traditional machinery for collective bargaining. . . ."[22]

In 1925, Miss Rathbone asked the N.U.S.E.C. to make support of the family Endowment Plan as one of its guiding principles. Dame Millicent Garrett Fawcett, founder and former president of the group, opposed the Plan as a serious threat to the strength of the family. Others in the N.U.S.E.C. questioned the wisdom of adding another cause to their principles until equal franchise for all adult women had been achieved. Miss Rathbone referred to members of this group as the "me, too" feminists who were only interested in copying men.[23] Miss Rathbone saw the need for a "New Feminism" where women would hold that "now that we have secured possession of the tools of citizenship, we intend to use them not to copy men's models but to produce our own."[24] She convinced the organization to support a plan that would place "the service of motherhood in the position of security and honour which it merits but can never reach under the present system."[25]

As various types of family allowance were used to meet national emergencies, supporters increased. Just as Government's payments to servicemen's families during World War I had been based on family size, statistics proved that families were better off economically during the Depression years, when "relief allowances are usually proportioned to the size of the family, which wages are not. . . ."[26] Furthermore, the population in Britain in the 1930s did begin to show a sharp decline— a decline that had been predicted if families did not receive financial help.

Writing in 1939, ten years after her first successful bid for a seat in the House of Commons, Miss Rathbone stated that "the main obstacle to the passage of a Family Endowment Plan was the stringency due to defense expenditures and the suspicious and aloof attitude of the official Labour Party and the T.U.C."[27] It was not until June 11, 1945, that her dream was realized and a Family Endowment Bill was passed. This was considered a great personal triumph for her, especially because she had rejected the first Plan proposed in Parliament that would have paid money to fathers rather than mothers.

Parliamentary Career: 1929-1946

Miss Rathbone was content to devote herself exclusively to the cause of British women's rights until she read Katharine Mayo's book *Mother India* in 1927. She attributed the appalling problems outlined in its pages—child marriages and lack of medical care during childbirth among them—to the failure of the British government to assume its responsibility for conditions in their colony. Her immediate response was a decision to stand again for Parliament. Her opportunity came in 1928 when she received a formal invitation to stand for one of the two seats representing the Combined English Universities. As an Independent, she received support from all parties in the General Election of 1929. Her supporters sent letters to University graduates asking for their votes and emphasizing the advantages of an Independent candidate. A special appeal was also made to women graduates, although not on feminist grounds, because Miss Rathbone "disclaimed that in her election address."[28]

Miss Rathbone sent a circular to the voters outlining her position on what she considered to be the most important issues. These were the same issues that continued to attract her interest throughout her long career. First, she was interested in education. New schools were needed and the size of the classes had to be reduced. She also believed that universities should be open to any child capable of attending, and that the parents of secondary school children attending private schools should not bear the double burden of school tuition and rates for the public schools. For her university constituents, she wanted Civil Service jobs made more readily available. The majority of public servants were "recruited at so early an age that University graduates are practically excluded."[29] Another major issue that affected university graduates was the proposed 1934 Unemployment Bill. This bill was in two parts. Part I concerned unemployment insurance, which would be based on the amount of contributions paid by the insured persons, the employers, and the Government. Part II created an Unemployment Assistance Board composed of six members. This board would also pay the unemployed additional money when a needs test showed this to be necessary; it would help those who had used up all their benefits; and it would award payment to any able-bodied unemployed who had no insurance, provided they were insured under the Widow's, Orphan's, and Old Age Contributory Pensions Act. But anyone who had earned over £250 per year was automatically excluded from the benefits of the proposed bill. This restriction tended to eliminate the university graduates.

Miss Rathbone sent out a questionnaire to her constituents in order to obtain a true picture of the job situation. One-fifth of those polled replied (4,327 out of a possible 22,399). Of these, 86% favored an increase in the income limit even though it meant a compulsory weekly contribution. (In 1936 the Government did raise the upper income limit to £400 per year for the Unemployment Assistance Board but refused to raise the limit for Unemployment Insurance.)

The problem of unemployment in Britain led Miss Rathbone into many related areas. She supported the public works plan, although she did not feel that they were extensive enough. She wanted to see production increased and fairer distributions of income achieved and considered the payment of allowances to dependent children a necessity. She organized and served as chairman of the Children's Minimum Campaign Committee. This all-party Committee lobbied to get the Government to agree in its 1934 Unemployment Bill that "no child should go short of the necessities of healthy upbringing merely because of its parents' poverty, and that the scale providing for these necessities should be based on scientific data."[30] In the previous year (March 27, 1934), she had led a deputation to the Minister of Labor that was concerned about the need to use "scientific and reasoned treatment" in setting sums to be given unemployed families for their children.[31] This group proposed that a committee should be set up by the Ministry of Health to consult medical authorities, economic experts, and housewives to determine children's nutritional needs and the amount of money needed to meet these needs. The amount to be paid would be based on a sliding scale reflecting the applicant's own resources.

The Children's Minimum Campaign Committee also succeeded in persuading the government to subsidize the provision of milk to English schoolchildren. By 1936 they were advocating free milk and school lunches for schoolchildren, as well as milk for pregnant mothers and preschool children, but these goals were not immediately realized.

Miss Rathbone also advocated slum clearance, with subsidized housing available for even the poorest citizens. She followed closely all Government actions relating to housing and was distressed by the 1933 Housing Act, because it stopped all Government subsidies except for slum clearance. Although the Government believed private enterprise would build the necessary houses, Miss Rathbone was skeptical.

The most potentially dangerous problem facing Britain in the 1930s was in the sphere of international affairs. Miss Rathbone supported the League of Nations as the only hope to achieve peace with security. She also supported Free Trade, viewing protection as a potential source of international strife.

Once elected to the House of Commons, a great deal of Miss Rathbone's energy was directed to the Indian question and to protecting the University seats. Labor led the fight to eliminate these seats. One of their charges was that these were simply safe Tory seats. Their effort was defeated by only four votes, with Miss Rathbone given the major credit. (The seats were abolished shortly after her death in 1946.)

Miss Rathbone's interest in the status of Indian women never wavered. In October 1927 she organized a meeting of women's organizations to discuss action and was selected to direct the National Union of Societies for Equal Citizenship in a study of the situation. There had been much publicity about the Indian traditions regarding widowhood, child marriages, and purdah, but Miss Rathbone was determined to gather the actual statistics. Indian women resented the actions of the committee and the resultant publicity because they felt that their own efforts to remedy the situation were ignored. In an effort to smooth the ruffled feelings of the Indian women, Miss Rathbone invited those residing in London to a tea. During the discussions, the group decided to call a conference. Again, ill-will was created because the Indian women were described as "advisors"; they again felt that they were being treated as inferiors. Furthermore, Miss Rathbone had brought Indian mistrust upon her actions because she had allowed Miss Mayo's name and book to be associated with her own efforts, and the Indians had been infuriated by the Mayo book because it not only brought discredit upon India, but also ignored the work of local Indian reformers.

At the same time that Miss Rathbone was engaged in her Indian efforts the British Government had appointed a Royal Commission under the chairmanship of Sir John Simon (later Viscount) to study constitutional reform for India. The Government of India Act of 1919 under which India was governed was to be revised in 1929, but because of general unrest a review was started in 1927. The Indians objected to the resultant Simon Commission because there were no Indians appointed to the Panel. By the time the Commission issued its report in 1930, Indian civil disobedience was at its height, and they refused to accept the report even for the purpose of discussion.

In 1930 the MacDonald Government summoned a Round Table Conference to devise a satisfactory compromise. Indians were included in the ninety members. All the members were agreed on the creation of a representative parliamentary system. Miss Rathbone immediately began to work toward universal suffrage, utilizing the techniques perfected by British suffragists.

The intense concern that Miss Rathbone felt over the political and social plight of Indian women naturally led her to visit India as soon as she felt free of her Parliamentary duties. During the Parliamentary Christmas recess (1931-1932) she left on an extended tour that lasted until Easter. She traveled on the same ship as the members of the Franchise Committee of the Round Table Commission. The Conservative M.P., Mary Pickford, was the official woman delegate with the Committee, but Miss Rathbone had also invited Hester Gray, who had lived in India, as her companion. She justified the trip because "of the all important stages in the granting of self-governing institutions to India foreshadowed for this year." She felt that she should "observe certain aspects of the problem for myself and also to get to know personally the leaders of the women's movement in India."[32] She planned to make contact with the leading Indian women and help them with the "political and technical realities of the franchise problem," as well as gain firsthand knowledge about the Indian traditions that were so detrimental to the well-being of Indian women.[33]

During the trip to India, Miss Rathbone described her impressions in letters that were circulated among her constituents. She was warned at the start of the trip by Mrs. Mackenzie, wife of the President of the Scotch College in India, that "the Indian ladies were very much on the defensive against suggestions from outside."[34] This advice was to prove correct. In February Miss Rathbone wrote that the Indian women were:

. . . personally polite, but very aloof. . . . We were told that they were determined to take nothing from English women,—and had a "mind your own business sort of attitude," while I personally was regarded as a spy and an "English Katharine Mayo!"[35]

This coolness and occasionally outright hostility from the Indian women did not dampen her enthusiasm. She returned to England convinced that India should be given its independence and admitted to the British Commonwealth of Nations, and that Indian women's rights must be guaranteed in the constitution in order to combat such evils as "child marriages, maltreated maternity, purdah, and illiteracy."[36]

To help publicize conditions in India throughout England, Miss Rathbone made many speeches and wrote a book on the evils of child marriages in 1935. She wanted to "kindle their [the British public's] imaginations and through these their emotions," because "for one man capable of reasoned thought there are a score who can only perceive and feel."[37]

Miss Rathbone was disturbed by the proposed Indian Constitution as set forth in the White Paper issued by the Government in 1934, because it only transferred "power from a few Englishmen to a few Indians."[38] However, the Committee she had helped organize for Indian women's franchise reaped its reward when their proposals were incorporated in the proposed Government of India Act. In 1938 India was given provincial autonomy; full independence did not come until 1947.

After winning her first General Election in 1929, Miss Rathbone had only two years to make an impact on her constituents before another election was called. The 1931 General Election proved to be a real contest. Miss Rathbone and the other M.P. (Sir Martin Conway) who represented the Combined English Universities were challenged by four aspirants. Although both incumbents were returned, Miss Rathbone recognized that "one of the few disadvantages of representing universities—is the rarity of the opportunities for coming face to face with one's constituency."[39] She decided to send an annual letter to her constituents in an effort to keep in touch, "a sort of personal account of my stewardship."[40] In her first letter, she described her trip to India and discussed her opposition to the Government's protectionist policy, its economy in education and housing, and her acceptance with misgivings of the budget. She discussed the injustices to women in the proposed Health Insurance Bill, as well as the question of Sunday entertainment (which she supported).

By 1934, Nazi successes in Germany had become a major international concern. In a resolution that received national attention members at the Oxford Union and later other university students declared that "under no circumstances will we fight for King and Country."[41] This led Miss Rathbone to prepare a Parliamentary statement that was, however, never delivered. In the undelivered speech, she explained that the students' position embraced three groups of opinion: "the ultra Pacifist," "those determined not to let their patriotism be exploited," and "those who would fight in a class war but not in a nationalist war." Although she tried to be understanding and not overly critical of the students, she was gravely concerned. In her annual letter to her constituents, she referred to the ambiguity of the document as a possible source of encouragement to possible aggressors. But she herself did not consider it unpatriotic.[42]

Popular with her constituents, Miss Rathbone was returned unopposed when another General Election was called in 1935. This was one of only three occasions when a woman was returned without having to fight an election.[43]

Throughout her Parliamentary career, Miss Rathbone was concerned about the condition of native women in the British colonies. Shortly after her election she joined the Duchess of Atholl's newly formed Committee for the Protection of Coloured Women in the Colonies. She was also keenly interested in the Zionist cause in Palestine and spent her summer holiday in 1935 visiting Palestine and Egypt. Upon her return to England, she proposed that a woman be appointed to the Palestine Commission. The Colonial Governor, William Ormsby-Gore (later Baron Harlech), "did not think its adoption would be practical."[44] Miss Rathbone opposed also the Government's proposal to withdraw the rights of Jewish women to vote or stand for municipal elections.[45] The Government denied that its proposal was a withdrawal of rights, because Palestinian women had never voted. Jewish women had been and were still allowed to vote in purely Jewish townships.[46]

In 1938, Miss Rathbone wrote *War Can Be Averted* (Victor Gollancz, 1938), in which she discussed her views on the world situation. The success of Italy in Abyssinia dismayed her, because she feared it would lead to "a far more general and terrible war."[47] The League of Nations, she contended, was still the world's only hope of averting a world disaster. The nations must join together and apply sanctions against Italy through the League. A nonintervention policy was helping Fascism, as was all talk of appeasement and disarmament.

As a result of her perception of the Nazi threat, Miss Rathbone voted for all increased Government arms expenditures. Sanctions would not be enough unless "the fascists know that force will be used if necessary."[48] She also believed that the British should initiate a closer relationship with the USSR to forestall the Germans.

Miss Rathbone made several trips to the continent during the 1930s. In 1937 she visited Spain, accompanied by the Duchess of Atholl, Dame Rachel Crowdy, and Ellen Wilkinson. She was very impressed with the courage of the Spaniards "in these days of defeatism."[49] In that same year she also went with the Duchess of Atholl on a three-week trip to Rumania, Yugoslavia, and Czechoslovakia. They traveled tirelessly, meeting and talking with all classes of citizens, from royalty to workers. They were fearful that the League would not support these countries' legitimate governments against aggression. She returned to Prague shortly before the war to aid in speeding the flow of refugees.

Miss Rathbone waged her own war against Germany. She wrote a letter to the Wayfarers Travel Agency, refusing to use their services because they had advertised travel in Germany.[50] On her own initiative, she proposed a recommendation later backed by a hundred M.P.s that Carl von Ossietzky, a German pacifist and publicist imprisoned in Germany, should be the recipient of the 1936 Nobel Peace Prize.[51] She held a prominent place on most of the committees set up to aid the refugees, serving as vice-chairman of the National Joint Committee for Spanish Relief. This was an all-party group that coordinated the various Spanish relief agencies. As noted in the chapter on the Duchess of Atholl, one of the more popular and successful projects was the raising of £300,000 to bring 4,000 Basque children to England to escape the seige of Bilbao. She was also an honorary secretary of a two-hundred-member all-party Parliamentary Committee on Refugees that tried to resettle European refugees. She served on the advisory committee of the Czech Refugee Trust and the Central Committee for Refugees. The Central Committee was organized to dispense Government grants to refugees from Europe.

Miss Rathbone condemned Britain's "neglect of defenses and reliance on appeasement," and its "half-hearted attempt at collective security"; these strengthened the Fascists while weakening Britain.[52] This weakness led Britain into the folly of not supporting Abyssinia, Czechoslovakia, Spain, and China, or the Jewish people in Palestine. As a result Britain would either face a massive war or "sink stage by stage into the position of a second-rate power."[53]

With the advent of the war Miss Rathbone turned her energy toward helping the country in every way possible. She favored compulsory war work for all women, opposing the exemption of married women, and she helped organize an All-Party Parliamentary Action Group "to hear experts and discuss problems which cannot from their nature be freely debated in the presence of public and press."[54] She served as a member of the Ministry of Pensions Advisory Committee, whose duties were to award pensions to disabled men and to the dependents of those killed in the war. As she had during World War I, Miss Rathbone served as chairman of the Liverpool Soldiers', Sailors' and Airmen's Families Association, which handled the Government's allowances for the dependents of servicemen.

The war brought new problems for Miss Rathbone's constituents. Keeping the universities running was a major problem, because both faculty and students were called for military service. Miss Rathbone had ambivalent feelings in regard to this problem. She definitely supported the premise that the universities must remain open, but the choice of candidates for deferment was a matter of grave concern to her.

With the successful conclusion of the war came the prospect of an immediate General Election. Miss Rathbone was undecided whether to make a last stand for Parliament. She wrote to various friends for advice, after carefully listing her own reasons for entertaining the idea. Basically, she felt that there were too few M.P.s who were interested enough to give much time to the problems of the refugees and to "family allowances and kindred services." Furthermore, there were "too few women in Parliament and I am the only woman University M.P."[55] Because it was rumored that she was planning to retire, Miss Rathbone wrote to Lady Violet Bonham Carter denying the rumor and seeking to learn the attitude of the Liberal Party toward her candidacy.[56] Lady Bonham Carter responded immediately: "No member of my Party shall oppose you while I have a vestige of power in its counsels—I regard you as one of the finest Liberals I know."[57]

That Miss Rathbone's constituents recognized her devoted service was made evident by the substantial majority that returned her to Parliament in the General Election of 1945. Although now seventy-three years of age, Miss Rathbone was physically strong and healthy. She continued her active pace as she turned to postwar problems. The two major issues that drew her attention were the problem of the European refugees and the future of Palestine. Her career was ended quite suddenly on January 1, 1946, when she suffered a fatal heart attack.

The greater part of her fortune Miss Rathbone left to charities. After her death a memorial fund was created to support an annual Eleanor Rathbone Lecture on social or political themes, to be given annually at either Somerville College, Oxford, or one of the universities that had been included in her combined English University constituency. The University of Liverpool has an Eleanor Rathbone Chair of Social Science, and the state of Israel, in appreciation for her support, named a center for cultural activities the Rathbone House.

Conclusion

Eleanor Rathbone's career had many elements that were typical of "Pioneer" women in both the Labor and Conservative parties. She was dedicated to the termination of inequality for women, whether legal, political, or economic. Her devotion to the cause of those who were vulnerable to economic and political oppression was at the center of her political life. Yet she herself was economically secure and began with many advantages unknown to a large number of her female colleagues in the Labor Party.

Although an early feminist, Miss Rathbone was not a militant. She believed that women had to become politicians in order to gain the vote, advancing ideas before opposition could be formed and willing to accept compromises. She herself was the only active suffragist to be elected to Parliament as an Independent. She lived to see three of her major objectives successfully implemented: an equal franchise for English women, an improved franchise for Indian women, and the enactment of a Family Allowance Plan. She summed up her own attitude to her career in 1939, writing that had she been told that she would be a "City Councillor, a Magistrate, a Member of Parliament, and LlS. of Liverpool University and a D.C.L. of Oxford, it would have seemed the most fantastic of prophecies."[58] Had she been William Rathbone VI's *son*, perhaps her political career would not have seemed "fantastic." Instead the tradition of Rathbone service had reached its culmination in a woman. Thus, to the already strong traditional concern for economic and social justice, a unique perception was added that left an indelible mark on the history of women's rights in England and throughout the British Empire.

Part Two:

THE ELECTORAL
PROCESS

4

Statistical Profile
of Women Members
of Parliament

To gain a sense of historical development, I divided the ninety-four women who were elected to the House of Commons between 1918 and 1970 into two groups. I dubbed Group I the "Pioneers"; this group contains the thirty-nine women elected to office in the seven general elections before 1945. These elections took place in 1918, 1922, 1923, 1924, 1929, 1931, and 1935. I dubbed Group II the "Moderns"; this group contains the fifty-five women elected in 1945 and in all succeeding general elections through 1970, a total of eight—1945, 1950, 1951, 1955, 1959, 1964, 1966, and 1970. (The years in which women M.P.s were elected to Parliament are recorded in Table 1.)

I chose 1945 as a dividing point because of its importance in British political history. No general election had been held in the previous ten years. As the first postwar election in England, it reflected the dislocations in social structure precipitated by the war. And it marked the culmination of the attempts by the Labor Party to gain a clear majority of the seats in Parliament.

The crucial date for British women was 1918. In that year, women over thirty were given the right to vote, after much agitation from the suffragist movement. Members of the militant Women's Social and Political Union (W.S.P.U.), which was founded by Emmeline Pankhurst in 1903, were active between 1909 and 1914, when World War I brought a halt to their work. The Representation of the People Act of 1918 was passed. Not until 1928, however, was the voting age for women lowered to twenty-one.

The 1918 election, the first in which women were candidates for Parliament, reflected the confused political situation. The Liberal Party had been in power since 1905, but because of the First World War a Coalition Government was formed under the leadership of Herbert Asquith, Liberal Party leader. By 1916, however, a Cabinet reshuffle was necessary and David Lloyd George became Prime Minister of the Second Coalition Government. This reshuffle split the Liberal Party,

51

TABLE 1

Distribution of Successful Women Candidates
for Parliament: 1918-1970

Year of General Election	Total Women Candidates	Women Elected				
		Total¹	Conservative	Party Labor	Liberal	Other
1918	17	1			*	1
1922	33	2	1*			1
1923	34	7	3	3*	1	
1924	41	4	3*	1		
1929	69	14	3	9*	1	1
1931	62	15	13*		1	1
1935	67	0	6*	1	1	1
1945	87	24	1	21*	1	1
1950	126	21	6	14*	1	
1951	77	17	6*	11		
1955	92	24	10*	14		
1959	81	25	12*	13		
1964	90	29	11	18*		
1966	81	26	7	19*		
1970	99	26	15*	10		1

(Left margin vertical labels: GROUP I PIONEERS for 1918–1935; GROUP II MODERNS for 1945–1970)

---

*Winning Party
¹Number include reelected candidates

SOURCE: See Appendix

leading Mr. Asquith's followers to form an Independent Liberal Party. So the election of 1918 saw a three-way contest between the Coalition Government, the Independent Liberal Party, and the Labor Party. The Coalition group under the leadership of the Liberal, Lloyd George, and the Conservative, Bonar Law, gained a clear majority. Of the next six elections before World War II, the Conservatives won four and the Labor Party only two. The Conservatives formed the government in 1922, 1924, 1931, and 1935; the Labor Party, in 1923 and 1929. In all, Conservatives controlled Parliament for twenty years between 1918 and 1945, and the Labor Party for only three. The Conservative years included the five-year wartime coalition government formed by Winston Churchill (1940-1945) and the four-year National Government formed by Ramsay MacDonald (1931-1935).

The thirty-nine Pioneers who served in Parliament during the period from 1918 to 1945 were divided by political party as follows: seventeen were Conservatives, sixteen were from the Labor Party, four were Liberals, one was an Independent, and one came from an Irish party (Sinn Fein; although elected, she didn't take her seat).

Between 1945 and 1970, the Conservative and Labor parties each won four general elections. The Conservatives, with wins in 1951, 1955, 1959, and 1970, dominated the House of Commons for fifteen years. The Labor Party, with wins in 1945, 1950, 1964, and 1966, was in control for twelve years. During this period, the Moderns were divided as follows: twenty-one were Conservatives, thirty-two were from the Labor Party, and the Scottish Nationalist and Independent Unity parties each were represented by one M.P.

In Group I the party that won the election had the largest group of women elected; but this was not true in Group II. In three of the eight elections, Labor did not win but still had more women elected than did the Conservatives (1951, 1955, and 1959, see Table 1). This reflects the fact that since 1918 the Labor Party has fielded more women candidates in each general election than the Conservatives or a total of 446 as compared to 270 for the Conservatives and 234 for the Liberals. But the Conservatives have allowed more women candidates to run for a seat presently held by the Conservatives than has the Labor Party, eighteen to twelve. Overall, neither party was generous to women. In an analysis of the elections held between 1918 and 1935, the *London Times* observed that "in the fifty-three constituencies contested by women, there had previously been twenty-seven wins by their own parties out of a possible 318. The male candidates, on the other hand, were contesting seats which their own parties had previously won in the proportion of sixty-one to 318."[1] The *Manchester Guardian* noted the same disparity in the 1950 election.[2]

Among the seventeen Conservative Pioneers, seven won seats previously occupied by their husbands. Two of the men had been killed during World War I. Another had been unseated because of "irregularities" on the part of his agent. The four remaining men were elevated to the peerage. All but one of the Conservative women replacing their husbands were titled when they entered Parliament. One of these, Muriel, Lady Gammans, ran for her husband's seat in 1957, after his death, because the seat had been held by a Gammans for the past twenty-five years. Even when she wanted to retire, in 1958, she was prevailed upon to continue, according to her friend, Joan, Lady Davidson.[3] She served for another eight years.

All of the women who replaced their husbands had taken active roles in their husbands' campaigns. According to the *Sunday Telegraph*, their successes were "proof of their ability to pass the test of being extremely well-known to the electors. All had been active workers in their husbands' constituencies, and had thereby gained valuable political experience."[4]

Joan, Lady Davidson, Conservative M.P. from 1937 to 1959, was one of the Pioneers who won her husband's seat when he entered the House of Lords. When a member of the selection committee asked her to stand for the seat, she was reluctant: home and family duties seemed too pressing. The committee persisted, in the person of a family friend, and Lady Davidson finally accepted the selection committee's nomination. During an interview in 1971, Lady Davidson took great pains to emphasize that the party's central selection committee did not have the final choice of nominees. Although they sent a list of suggested nominees to local constituency organizations, the final selections were made by the groups themselves. Nor did the national party organization put any pressure on local groups to accept its choices, according to Lady Davidson.[5]

Only two of the sixteen Labor Pioneers won seats previously occupied by their husbands. Lady Noel Buxton replaced her husband when he entered the House of Lords, and Agnes Hardie ran for her husband's seat (George Hardie) after his death. A third, Ruth Dalton, ran in a by-election as a stand-in for her husband. Hugh Dalton, an M.P. from Peckham, had announced his intention of contesting the Bishop Auckland seat at the next general election (1929). When the Labor M.P. from Bishop Auckland died suddenly, Mrs. Dalton ran in the by-election. She retired in favor of her husband in the next general election.

Among the thirty-two Labor Moderns, only one M.P. succeeded her husband. In a 1953 by-election, the recently widowed Lena Jeger won a hotly contested election.

Why were relatively few Labor women allowed to stand for safe seats, despite the large number of Labor women candidates? Lucy Middleton, Labor M.P. from 1945 to 1951, suggested that the influential trade unions simply preferred male candidates.[6] Lena Jeger, Labor M.P.

from 1953 to 1959 and again since 1964, also believes that trade unions have had a negative effect on women's political careers. Unions prefer candidates who came from their own ranks, she said, and women seem less and less interested in taking this route to a political career, often because of family commitments. Although the party need not accept union-sponsored candidates, she said, the unions make money available to "their own."[7]

During the modern era, however, trade unions seem to have lost some of their influence in selecting candidates for Parliament. Between 1918 and 1945, M.P.s who had been sponsored by trade unions outnumbered those candidates who ran without union support, in every election except one (1929). Since 1945, however, winning M.P.s running without union support have outnumbered those sponsored by trade unions in every election. For example, in 1935, seventy-eight of the 145 winning candidates were sponsored by trade unions, whereas by 1966 trade unions backed only 127 of the 345 winning candidates.[8]

Taking note of the unions' declining influence, Edith, Lady Summerskill (Labor M.P. from 1938 to 1955 and now a member of the House of Lords) cited her own daughter as an example. When Shirley Summerskill was proposed by the party's selection committee for Halifax, a wool-growing area, Lady Summerskill was skeptical about her chances for success. But on the basis of a speech made to the local committee, her daughter was nominated (and later elected, in 1964) to represent the district. Lady Summerskill commented that this would never have happened in the 1930s when she was beginning her own political career. She added that the party seems willing to accept candidates on their own merits, although women candidates must still be more capable than their male counterparts.[9]

An earlier observer shared Lady Summerskill's view: "In too many cases, a woman is chosen to fight for forlorn hope. To get more than a bare fighting chance, she must have exceptional ability or much personal charm or an unusually big pull behind the scene."[10]

The statistics suggest that women affiliated with the Labor Party have a better chance of becoming candidates for Parliament, but that Conservative women who become candidates have a better chance of being elected. Fourteen percent of all Conservative women candidates won seats in Parliament between 1918 and 1970, as compared to eleven percent of all Labor women candidates. (Successful candidates from both parties will be compared with unsuccessful candidates in chapter 5.)

Characteristics of Women M.P.s

To give a picture of these women M.P.s, I chose the following characteristics: age when elected to Parliament; education; occupation; family situation; and political experience. (Note that some of the percentages do not total 100 because of rounding.)

TABLE 2

Age of Women M.P.s When Elected

A. All Political Parties*

	Number		Percent	
	Group I	Group II	Group I	Group II
Age	(Pioneers)	(Moderns)	(Pioneers)	(Moderns)
20-29	2	1	6	2
30-39	13	20	39	38
40-49	12	16	36	30
50-59	5	14	15	27
60-69	1	2	3	4
	33	53	99	101

*Information missing for 6 Pioneers and 2 Moderns

B. Labor Party*

	Number		Percent	
	Group I	Group II	Group I	Group II
Age	(Pioneers)	(Moderns)	(Pioneers)	(Moderns)
20-29	1	—	8	—
30-39	5	11	42	37
40-49	2	7	17	23
50-59	3	10	25	33
60-69	1	2	8	7
	12	30	100	100

*Information missing for 4 Pioneers and 2 Moderns

C. Conservative Party*

	Number		Percent	
	Group I	Group II	Group I	Group II
Age	(Pioneers)	(Moderns)	(Pioneers)	(Moderns)
20-29	—	—	—	—
30-39	6	9	37	43
40-49	10	8	62	38
50-59	—	4	—	19
60-69	—	—	—	—
	16	21	99	100

*Information missing for 1 Pioneer

SOURCE: See Appendix

AGE

Bernadette Devlin, perhaps the most widely publicized woman candidate in 1969, was elected to represent Ulster, Northern Ireland, at the age of twenty-one. Whereas the oldest elected woman M.P. was Dr. Ethel Bentham at sixty-eight in 1929.

The average age of the Pioneers was forty-two; of the Moderns, forty-four. Lucy Middleton suggests, however, that many of the women who were candidates in 1945 might have run earlier had there been a general election during the war. The ten-year interval between general elections prevented normal political development for all potential candidates.[11] The average age of women M.P.s winning their first election in 1945 was fifty. If we remove this subgroup from Group II, the average age of the Moderns becomes forty-two—identical with the Pioneers.

The average age of women M.P.s from the Labor Party has steadily increased. Among the Pioneers, the average was forty-four; among Moderns, forty-seven. Because all the women elected to Parliament in 1945 were from the Labor Party, the high average of that one election naturally affected the overall Group II average. Without the 1945 subgroup, the average age for Labor Moderns was forty-five.

For the Conservatives, the average age was slightly lower than the overall average and the Labor average: forty-one for the Pioneers and forty-three for the Moderns. In the 1970 election, the average age of the nine new women M.P.s was forty-four. Eight of the nine were Conservatives, with an average age of forty-three, the same as the average for Conservative Moderns. The ninth woman, a Labor M.P., was fifty-one.

EDUCATION

Among the Pioneers, 44% were educated in private schools, 31% in state schools, and 25% in their own homes with private tutors. In other words, 69% were educated in a "privileged" environment. Among the Moderns, there is a different configuration. Although 40% attended private school, only 2% were tutored in their own homes. The majority, 57%, attended state schools.

It should be noted that secondary school information is lacking for thirty-six of the ninety-four women who served between 1918 and 1970. Missing are records for twenty-three (59%) of the thirty-nine Pioneers, and thirteen (24%) of the fifty-five Moderns. The fact that more Moderns provided this information in their official biographies is probably a reflection of the increasingly important role that education has come to play in English life.

Among the Labor women for whom statistics are available, the

TABLE 3

Secondary School Education for Women M.P.s

A. *All Political Parties**

	Number		Percent	
Type of Schooling	Group I (Pioneers)	Group II (Moderns)	Group I (Pioneers)	Group II (Moderns)
State School	5	24	31	57
Private School	7	17	44	40
Home Tutors	4	1	25	2
Total	*16*	*42*	*100*	*99*

_____

*Information missing for 23 Pioneers and 13 Moderns

B. *Labor Party**

	Number		Percent	
Type of Schooling	Group I (Pioneers)	Group II (Moderns)	Group I (Pioneers)	Group II (Moderns)
State School	4	16	67	69
Private School	2	6	33	26
Home Tutors	0	1	0	4
Total	*6*	*23*	*100*	*99*

_____

*Information missing for 10 Pioneers and 9 Moderns

C. *Conservative Party**

	Number		Percent	
Type of Schooling	Group I (Pioneers)	Group II (Moderns)	Group I (Pioneers)	Group II (Moderns)
State School	1	7	13	39
Private School	4	11	50	61
Home Tutors	3	0	37	0
Total	*8*	*18*	*100*	*100*

_____

*Information missing for 9 Pioneers and 3 Moderns

SOURCE: See Appendix

changes were not dramatic. For the Pioneers, 67% of those reporting attended state schools and 33% attended private schools. Among Moderns, 69% of those reporting attended state schools and 26% attended private schools.

For Conservative M.P.s the changes were greater. Among Pioneers, 13% of those reporting attended state schools and 50% attended private schools. Among Moderns, 39% of those reporting attended state schools and 61% attended private schools. The greatest change occurred in the percentage educated in their homes: a drop from 37% to zero.

More Moderns than Pioneers attended institutions of higher learning. For the Labor women, however, there is no change in the percentages. It is among Conservative women M.P.s that changes have occurred. But the figures for Conservatives must be evaluated with caution, because information is missing for nine of the seventeen Pioneers. Statistics for college and university enrollment are presented separately because they are primarily training centers for one particular profession—e.g., teaching.

Among Pioneers, seven percent attended colleges and 52% attended universities. Among Moderns, 21% attended colleges and 44% attended universities. Seven percent of the Pioneers and six percent of the Moderns were educated in colleges and universities abroad. Among the Pioneers, then 66% had attended institutions of higher learning in England or abroad. Among the Moderns, this was true for 71%.

More Labor Pioneers attended universities (down from 69% to 50% among Moderns), but at the same time there was an increase in the women attending teacher-training colleges (from six percent to 25%). The result is that the total percentage of Labor Women receiving a higher education is the same in both groups: 75%.

The picture is quite different among Conservative women. Of those Pioneers who reported (less than half), 13% attended universities; none attended college; and 13% were educated abroad. Among the Moderns, 32% attended universities, 18% attended college, and another 14% were educated in colleges and universities abroad. In other words, 26% of the Conservative Pioneers and 64% of the Moderns received a higher education.

OCCUPATION

Among the Pioneers, 39% held salaried political positions, as elected office holders, union organizers, or civil servants. Only 29% came from the professions or business. Another 32% were unemployed. Some unemployed women who were elected to Parliament had devoted most of their time to home and family before the election. Others, however, were wealthy women whose homes were cared for by servants. Many of these wealthy women had active political careers before entering Par-

TABLE 4

Higher Education of Women M.P.s

A. *All Political Parties**

Type of Institution	Number		Percent	
	Group I (Pioneers)	Group II (Moderns)	Group I (Pioneers)	Group II (Moderns)
University	15	23	52	44
College	2	11	7	21
Abroad†	2	3	7	6
None	10	15	34	29
Total	29	52	100	100

---

*Information missing for 10 Pioneers and 3 Moderns
†Attended university or college in another country

B. *Labor Party**

Type of Institution	Number		Percent	
	Group I (Pioneers)	Group II (Moderns)	Group I (Pioneers)	Group II (Moderns)
University	11	14	69	50
College	1	7	6	25
Abroad†	0	0	0	0
None	4	7	25	25
Total	16	28	100	100

---

*Information missing for 4 Moderns
†Attended university or college in another country

C. *Conservative Party**

Type of Institution	Number		Percent	
	Group I (Pioneers)	Group II (Moderns)	Group I (Pioneers)	Group II (Moderns)
University	1	7	13	32
College	0	4	0	18
Abroad†	1	3	13	14
None	6	7	75	36
Total	8	21	101	100

---

*Information missing for 9 Pioneers
†Attended university or college in another country

SOURCE: See Appendix

TABLE 5

Occupations of Women M.P.s

A. *All Political Parties*

Occupation	Number Group I (Pioneers)	Group II (Moderns)	Percent Group I (Pioneers)	Group II (Moderns)
Political*	16	8	39	15
Professional/ Business†	12	35	29	66
Not employed	11	10	32	19
Total	39	53	100	100

*Elected office holders, union organizers, and civil servants.
†Professions include law, teaching, journalism, medicine, and theater. Positions in business are at the management level.

B. *Labor Party*

Occupation	Number Group I (Pioneers)	Group II (Moderns)	Percent Group I (Pioneers)	Group II (Moderns)
Political*	7	4	44	13
Professional/ Business†	5	21	31	66
Not employed	4	7	25	22
Total	16	32	100	101

*Elected office holders, union organizers, and civil servants.
†Professions include law, teaching, journalism, medicine, and theater. Positions in business are at the management level.

C. *Conservative Party*

Occupation	Number Group I (Pioneers)	Group II (Moderns)	Percent Group I (Pioneers)	Group II (Moderns)
Political*	4	4	24	19
Professional/ Business†	5	13	29	62
Not employed	8	4	47	19
Total	17	21	100	100

*Elected office holders, union organizers, and civil servants.
†Professions include law, teaching, journalism, medicine, and theater. Positions in business are at the management level.

SOURCE: See Appendix

liament, although they did not hold salaried positions. Among the Pioneers, the 32% unemployed were divided 20% to 12%, with the wealthy women the larger group. Among the Moderns, the 19% unemployed were divided 2% to 17%, with wealthy unemployed women the smaller group.

The swing toward the professions and business is clear among Moderns, with 66% engaged in medicine, journalism, law, teaching, and industry. The greatest increases came in journalism and business, with a slight decline in the number of M.P.s from medicine.

A relatively small number of the Moderns who entered Parliament had been employed in political positions (15%), as compared with the Pioneers. Although the civil service had gradually been opening its doors to women and more women had been elected to political office (Table 11-A), fewer women are working in the trade unions. Pioneers like Margaret Bondfield, Jennie Lee, and Ellen Wilkinson used their union activity as a springboard for their political careers, but fewer Moderns have taken this route.

Labor Pioneers were divided between political and professional/business occupations, with 44% in political life and 31% in a profession. But 66% of the Labor Moderns held political jobs, a result of their declining trade union activity. In all, 74% of the Labor Pioneers and 79% of the Labor Moderns had been employed before election to Parliament.

Among Conservatives, the striking change is in the number of women holding salaried positions before election, up from 53% of the Pioneers to 81% of the Moderns. There was a decline in the number in political occupations (from 24% of the Pioneers to 19% of the Moderns), and a shift in the number in the professions and industry (from 29% of the Pioneers to 62% of the Moderns). A breakdown of the professional figures reveals that no Conservative Pioneers came from careers in teaching or law. Both fields are represented among the Moderns.

FAMILY SITUATION

For all women M.P.s, there was an increase in the percentage of married women (49% to 56%) and widows (12% to 18%) among the Moderns, with a corresponding decline in the number of women who were single. The trend in the Labor Party follows the overall pattern, with an increase from Group I to Group II of married women (44% to 69%) and widows (6% to 16%), and a decline in the number of single women (50% to 16%). Conservative women, on the other hand, do not follow the overall trend. There are fewer married women in Group II than in Group I (from 53% down to 38%), and an increase

TABLE 6

Marital Status of Women M.P.s at Time of
First Election to Parliament

A. All Political Parties

Marital Status	Number		Percent	
	Group I (Pioneers)	Group II (Moderns)	Group I (Pioneers)	Group II (Moderns)
Married	19	31	49	56
Widowed	5	10	12	18
Single*	15	14	38	26
Total	39	55	99	100

*Includes two M.P.s who were married for the first time during their terms (e.g., Jenny Lee, Labor M.P. from 1929 to 1931, 1945—, and Thelma Cazalet-Keir, Conservative M.P. from 1931 to 1945, are listed in the "single" group).

B. Labor Party

Marital Status	Number		Percent	
	Group I (Pioneers)	Group II (Moderns)	Group I (Pioneers)	Group II (Moderns)
Married	7	22	44	69
Widowed	1	5	6	16
Single*	8	5	50	16
Total	16	32	100	101

*M.P.s who were unmarried at beginning of their terms and married while in Parliament are listed as "single."

C. Conservative Party

Marital Status	Number		Percent	
	Group I (Pioneers)	Group II (Moderns)	Group I (Pioneers)	Group II (Moderns)
Married	9	8	53	38
Widowed	3	5	18	24
Single*	5	8	29	38
Total	17	21	100	100

*M.P.s who were unmarried at beginning of their term and married while in Parliament are listed as "single."

SOURCE: See Appendix

in the number of unmarried women (from 29% to 38%). The increase in the number of Conservative widows elected to Parliament (from 19% to 24%) follows the overall trend.

If the percentages of widows and single women are combined, an important difference between Labor and Conservative women M.P.s is revealed. Among the Moderns, 32% of the Labor M.P.s are not married, as compared with 62% of the Conservatives.

Women who are members of Parliament are inevitably asked about their own and their families' attitudes toward their political careers. Here are some of their responses:

> I have asked myself whether it is either possible or desirable to try to continue the most loyal service to the House combined with the insistent claims of a distant constituency and the appeal of one's own children. Frankly, I say it is not.[12]

> [I cannot] indefinitely be a competent member of Parliament and successful mother to young children.[13]

> Domestic arrangements are always a bother . . . but you cope. Now our household is a cooperative affair. We all pitch in with the cooking and so on.[14]

A career in Parliament is particularly difficult for women whose home is far from London. Writing in the *Christian Science Monitor* of August 19, 1947, Melita Spraggs described the problems of Lady Priscilla Grant, Conservative M.P. from Aberdeen, Scotland.

> The girls are in boarding school and Lady Grant gets away once in two weeks to her constituency, and for a glimpse of her children. She travels all Thursday night and devotes Friday to her constituency. Saturday, she visits with her daughters but continues conferences. The girls "sleep at home only during holidays and half term." She returns to London on Sunday.

Despite these difficulties, Lady Grant served for twenty years. And it is interesting to note that 56% of the Moderns had one or more children, as compared with 39% of the Pioneers.

Among the Pioneers for whom family statistics are available, 41% were not married, 19% were married without children, 16% were married or widowed with small families (one or two children), and 23% were married or widowed and had large families (three to six children). Among the Moderns for whom family statistics are available, 29% were unmarried, 16% were married without children, 38% were married or widowed and had small families, and 18% were married or widowed and had large families.

A number of comparisons can be made between Pioneers and Mod-

TABLE 7

Women M.P.s With Children

A. *All Political Parties**

| | Number | | Percent | |
| | Group I | Group II | Group I | Group II |
Size of Family	(Pioneers)	(Moderns)	(Pioneers)	(Moderns)
Not Married	13	13	41	29
Married—No Children	6	7	19	16
Married or Widowed with 1 or 2 children	5	17	16	38
Married or Widowed with 3 to 6 children	7	8	23	18
Total	*31*	*45*	*99*	*101*

*Information missing for 8 Pioneers and 9 Moderns.

B. *Labor Party**

| | Number | | Percent | |
| | Group I | Group II | Group I | Group II |
Size of Family	(Pioneers)	(Moderns)	(Pioneers)	(Moderns)
Not Married	7	5	47	20
Married—No Children	3	5	20	20
Married or Widowed with 1 or 2 children	3	11	20	44
Married or Widowed with 3 to 6 children	2	4	13	16
Total	*15*	*25*	*100*	*100*

*Information missing for 1 Pioneer and 7 Moderns

C. *Conservative Party**

| | Number | | Percent | |
| | Group I | Group II | Group I | Group II |
Size of Family	(Pioneers)	(Moderns)	(Pioneers)	(Moderns)
Not Married	4	8	29	40
Married—No Children	3	3	21	15
Married or Widowed with 1 or 2 children	2	5	14	25
Married or Widowed with 3 to 6 children	5	4	36	20
Total	*14*	*20*	*100*	*100*

*Information missing for 3 Pioneers and 1 Modern.

SOURCE: *See* Appendix

erns. These comparisons tend to reflect the similarity of the women politicians to their own society. As has already been noted, there are fewer single women among the Moderns. A majority (60%) of the Pioneers had no children, while a majority of the Moderns (56%) had one or more. Large families were more prevalent among Pioneers; smaller families among Moderns. Indeed, the largest subgroup among Moderns consists of women with one or two children. Among the Pioneers, the largest subgroup is made up of single women. In both Group I and Group II, there are more married women and widows with children than without.

It has already been noted that more Labor Pioneers were single women than is true for Labor Moderns. Also, we find that only 33% of the Labor Pioneers had one or more children, compared with 60% of the Moderns. The largest subgroup among Labor Pioneers is made up of single women, while, among Moderns, the largest subgroup consists of women with small families. For both Pioneers and Moderns, there are fewer women with large families than with small. A majority of all married and widowed Labor M.P.s have children.

Conservative M.P.s do not conform to the general trends among women M.P.s from all political parties. As noted earlier, there are more single Conservative women among the Moderns than among the Pioneers. Grouping single women with married women without children, we find that 50% of the Pioneers and 55% of the Moderns were childless. Among all Conservative Pioneers, the largest subgroup is unmarried. Among married and widowed Moderns, a majority have children, and small families outnumber large families.

For married Pioneers, the majority of husbands were involved in some aspect of political life: as M.P.s, members of the House of Lords, or party workers. Twenty-six percent of the husbands of Pioneers were in the professions; another 11% were in industry. No husbands held unskilled jobs. Among the married Moderns, the percentage of husbands in industry was the highest (39%), and the percent holding political positions was down to 23%, the lowest of all categories except for unskilled workers.

The husbands of married Labor Pioneers were divided between two categories: political (72%) and professional (29%). The married Moderns' husbands were far more diverse: professionals led with 39%; politicians declined to 33%. Men in industry (17%) and unskilled workers (11%) appeared for the first time.

Changes in the occupations of husbands are equally dramatic for Conservative women. Political occupations account for 44% of the husbands of married Pioneers, followed by the professions (33%) and industry (22%). There are *no* husbands in politics for the married Moderns, while 83% are in industry. The remaining 17% are in the professions.

POLITICAL EXPERIENCE

How often did women M.P.s run for seats in Parliament before they were successful? Among the thirty-nine Pioneers, 63% won in their first campaigns. This was true for only 43% of the Moderns. Among the Pioneers, 18% won office on their second attempts, compared with 30% of the Moderns. Third-time winners were almost even in the two groups: 16% of the Pioneers and 15% of the Moderns. Only a small percentage of the Pioneers (3%) entered Parliament after three unsuccessful campaigns. Thirteen percent of the Moderns entered Parliament on their fourth or fifth attempts. In summary, a majority of Pioneers and Moderns were successful on their first attempt to enter Parliament. But, for the Pioneers, chances of winning a seat on the second or subsequent attempts were markedly down. More than half the Moderns, on the other hand, won seats after one or more unsuccessful attempts.

Among Labor Pioneers, more were successful on their third try (25%) than their second (19%), although half had succeeded on their first. More Labor Moderns succeeded on their second attempts (39%) than on their first (36%). The remaining 28% made two to five unsuccessful bids before winning an election.

Eighty-one percent of the Conservative Pioneers were first-time winners. This is probably a reflection of the large number who took over their husbands' seats. Only 6% won on second attempts, and slightly more (13%) on their third. No successful candidate had gone further than this. Among Conservative Moderns, 48% won on their first efforts; 19% on their second, 19% on their third, and 14% on their fourth or fifth. More than half, then, withstood unsuccessful campaigns and made repeated efforts to gain a seat in Parliament.

An analysis of the family background of women M.P.s reveals significant differences between Pioneers and Moderns. What percentage came from families whose political activities may have influenced their daughters' or wives' careers? Among the Pioneers, the figures are the most clearcut. Thirty-three percent of the women were elected to replace their husbands and another 8% had husbands who were M.P.s before or during their wives' terms. Fifteen percent had fathers who were M.P.s[15] as well as 5% had brothers who were M.P.s.[16] Because one of the brothers also had a father who was an M.P., we find 59% of the women had ties to Parliament before they themselves were elected. Another 13% came from families active in some aspect of politics.

The importance of family orientation drops considerably for the Moderns. Only one took over her husband's seat.[17] Another was elected to her father's seat.[18] And Shirley Summerskill was the daughter of a Pioneer—surely the sign of changing times. (Edith, Lady Summerskill is now a life peeress.) Less than half of all Moderns (44%) came from

TABLE 8

Husbands' Occupations

A. *All Political Parties*＊

| | Number | | Percent | |
Occupation	Group I (Pioneers)	Group II (Moderns)	Group I (Pioneers)	Group II (Moderns)
Politics[1]	12	6	63	23
Professions[2]	5	8	26	31
Industry[3]	2	10	11	39
Unskilled Worker	0	2	0	8
Total	*19*	*26*	*100*	*101*

＊Information missing on 5 Moderns

B. *Labor Party*＊

| | Number | | Percent | |
Occupation	Group I (Pioneers)	Group II (Moderns)	Group I (Pioneers)	Group II (Moderns)
Politics[1]	5	6	72	33
Professions[2]	2	7	29	39
Industry[3]	0	3	0	17
Unskilled Worker	0	2	0	11
Total	*7*	*18*	*101*	*100*

＊Information missing for 4 Moderns

C. *Conservative Party*＊

| | Number | | Percent | |
Occupation	Group I (Pioneers)	Group II (Moderns)	Group I (Pioneers)	Group II (Moderns)
Politics[1]	4	0	44	0
Professions[2]	3	1	33	17
Industry[3]	2	5	22	83
Unskilled Worker	0	0	0	0
Total	*9*	*6*	*99*	*100*

＊Information missing for 2 Moderns
[1]Includes members of the House of Commons, the House of Lords, and workers in party organizations.
[2]Includes physicians, lawyers, artists, journalists, and teachers.
[3]Includes scientists, accountants, business managers, and engineers.

SOURCE: *See* Appendix

TABLE 9

*Women M.P.s: Number of Bids for Parliament
Before First Success*

A. All Political Parties

Number of Unsuccessful Campaigns	Number		Percent	
	Group I (Pioneers)	Group II (Moderns)	Group I (Pioneers)	Group II (Moderns)
None	24	23	63	43
One	7	16	18	30
Two	6	8	16	15
Three to five	1	7	3	13
Total	*38*	*54*	*100*	*101*

B. Labor Party

Number of Unsuccessful Campaigns	Number		Percent	
	Group I (Pioneers)	Group II (Moderns)	Group I (Pioneers)	Group II (Moderns)
None	8	11	50	36
One	3	12	19	39
Two	4	4	25	13
Three to five	1	4	6	13
Total	*16*	*31*	*100*	*101*

C. Conservative Party

Number of Unsuccessful Campaigns	Number		Percent	
	Group I (Pioneers)	Group II (Moderns)	Group I (Pioneers)	Group II (Moderns)
None	13	10	81	48
One	1	4	6	19
Two	2	4	13	19
Three to five	0	3	0	14
Total	*16*	*21*	*100*	*100*

SOURCE: *See* Appendix

TABLE 10

Political Activity of Women M.P.s' Families

A.   *All Political Parties*

	Number		Percent	
	Group I	Group II	Group I	Group II
Relationship	(Pioneers)	(Moderns)	(Pioneers)	(Moderns)
HUSBAND				
Former M.P.				
(Succeeded by Wife)	13	1	33	4
M.P. before and/or				
during wife's term	3	3	8	5
Never an M.P.	23	51	59	91
Total	39	55	100	100
FATHER OR MOTHER*				
Former M.P. (Suc-				
ceeded by Daughter)	0	1	0	2
M.P. before and/or during				
daughter's term	6	2*	15	4
Never an M.P.	33	52	85	94
Total	39	55	100	100
BROTHER				
M.P.	2	0	5	0
Never an M.P.	37	55	95	100
Total	39	55	100	100
Family Active in Politics	28	24	72	44
Family Not Active				
in Politics	11	31	28	56
Total	39	55	100	100

*One Modern, Shirley Summerskill, is the daughter of a Pioneer, Lady Edith Summerskill.

SOURCE: *See* Appendix

B.   *Labor Party*

	Number		Percent	
	Group I	Group II	Group I	Group II
Relationship	(Pioneers)	(Moderns)	(Pioneers)	(Moderns)
HUSBAND				
Former M.P.				
(Succeeded by Wife)	3	1	19	3
M.P. before and/or				
during wife's term	3	3	19	9
Never an M.P.	10	28	63	88
Total	16	32	101	100

TABLE 10 *(Continued)*

B. *Labor Party*

Relationship	Number		Percent	
	Group I (Pioneers)	Group II (Moderns)	Group I (Pioneers)	Group II (Moderns)....
FATHER OR MOTHER*				
Former M.P. (Succeeded by Daughter)	0	0	0	0
M.P. before and/or during daughter's term	1	2*	6	6
Never an M.P.	15	30	94	94
Total	*16*	*32*	*100*	*100*
Family Active in Politics	10	16	63	50
Family Not Active in Politics	6	16	36	50
Total	*16*	*32*	*99*	*100*

*One Modern, Shirley Summerskill, is the daughter of a Pioneer, Lady Edith Summerskill.

SOURCE: *See* Appendix

C. *Conservative Party*

Relationship	Number		Percent	
	Group I (Pioneers)	Group II (Moderns)	Group I (Pioneers)	Group II (Moderns)
HUSBAND				
Former M.P. (Succeeded by Wife)	8	0	47	5
M.P. before and/or during wife's term	0	0	0	0
Never an M.P.	9	21	53	95
Total	*17*	*21*	*100*	*100*
FATHER				
Former M.P. (Succeeded by Daughter)	0	1	0	5
M.P. before and/or after daughter's term	2	1	12	5
Never an M.P.	15	19	88	90
Total	*17*	*21*	*100*	*100*
BROTHER				
M.P. before and/or during sister's term	1	0	6	0
Never an M.P.	16	21	94	100
Total	*17*	*21*	*100*	*100*
Family Active in Politics	12	8	71	38
Family Not Active in Politics	5	13	29	63
Total	*17*	*21*	*100*	*101*

SOURCE: *See* Appendix

TABLE 11

Previous Public Offices Held by Women M.P.s

A. *All Political Parties*

	Number		Percent	
	Group I	Group II	Group I	Group II
Elected Office	(Pioneers)	(Moderns)	(Pioneers)	(Moderns)
Mayor	0	2	0	4
Local Government	11	32	22	57
Suffragist Movement	9	0	18	0
None	29	22	59	39
Total	*49*	*56*	*99*	*100*

B. *Labor Party*

	Number		Percent	
	Group I	Group II	Group I	Group II
Elected Office	(Pioneers)	(Moderns)	(Pioneers)	(Moderns)
Mayor	0	1	0	3
Local Government	6	19	26	59
Suffragist Movement	7	0	31	0
None	10	12	44	38
Total	*23*	*32*	*101*	*100*

C. *Conservative Party*

	Number		Percent	
	Group I	Group II	Group I	Group II
Elected Office	(Pioneers)	(Moderns)	(Pioneers)	(Moderns)
Mayor	0	1	0	5
Local Government	2	13	11	59
Suffragist Movement	1	0	6	0
None	15	8	83	36
Total	*18*	*22*	*100*	*100*

SOURCE: *See* Appendix

families with some political background, and only 14% were related to M.P.s.

Among Labor Pioneers, 19% had husbands who were serving in Parliament, and another 19% took over their husbands' seats. Among the Moderns, one woman took over her husband's seat and three women had husbands who were also M.P.s, a total of 12%. The number of Labor M.P.s with family members active in any kind of political activity declined from 63% in Group I to 50% in Group II.

Statistics for Conservative women with politically active families change considerably from Group I to Group II. Among the Conservative Pioneers, 47% were replacing their husbands; this was true for *one* of the Moderns. One Modern, Patricia Ford, ran for her father's seat after

TABLE 12

Political Party Experience of Women M.P.s

A. *All Political Parties*

Party Experience	Number Group I (Pioneers)	Group II (Moderns)	Percent Group I (Pioneers)	Group II (Moderns)
Worker	20	19	38	21
Officer	4	19	8	21
Women's Section	10	7	19	8
National Executive Board	7	12	13	13
Other	7	26	13	29
No Experience	5	7	10	8
Total	*53*	*90*	*101*	*100*

B. *Labor Party*

Party Experience	Number Group I (Pioneers)	Group II (Moderns)	Percent Group I (Pioneers)	Group II (Moderns)
Worker	8	8	29	15
Office	3	7	11	13
Women's Section	4	4	14	7
National Executive Board	6	9	21	17
Union Officer	2	1	7	2
Co-op Party	1	14	4	26
Fabian Society	3	8	11	15
No Experience	1	3	2	6
Total	*28*	*54*	*99*	*101*

C. *Conservative Party*

Party Experience	Number Group I (Pioneers)	Group II (Moderns)	Percent Group I (Pioneers)	Group II (Moderns)
Worker	9	10	53	30
Officer	1	11	6	33
Women's Section	3	3	18	8
National Executive Board	1	2	6	6
Comm. 1922	1	3	6	9
No Experience	2	4	12	12
Total	*17*	*33*	*101*	*98*

SOURCE: See Appendix

his death. The number of women with families active in some aspect of politics declined from 71% to 38%. To sum up, more Conservative Members were self-starters, entering the political arena without the backing of influential families.

As more women became involved in the political process, the importance of the individual's political experience seems to supplant family influence. Only 22% of the Pioneers had been elected to public office, a fact that is hardly surprising given their recent entry into the political sphere. Another 18% were involved in the Suffragist movement. Among the Moderns, only 39% had never been elected to any office. Of the 61% who had held office, 4% had served as mayors.

Among the Labor M.P.s, 26% of the Pioneers and 62% of the Moderns had held elected office. Another 31% of the Pioneers had been active in the Suffragist movement.

Conservative Pioneers were far less politically sophisticated than their Labor sisters. Only 11% had been elected to office and one woman had been active in the Suffragist movement. Conservative Moderns were different: 64% had experience in local government, including one who had served as a mayor. Only 36% of the Moderns had never been elected to office before entering Parliament.

Most of the women M.P.s had participated in some type of activity within their political parties. Only 10% of the Pioneers and 8% of the Moderns lacked any party experience. The most noticeable change between the two groups was in the number of women who had worked in the women's section of their parties, a drop from 19% to 8%. This may reflect the women's ambitions to develop their own independent political careers rather than to serve in supportive positions for their husbands and other male candidates. Among both Pioneers and Moderns, 13% served as members of the national executive boards of their parties; that is, as policy makers.

The trends for Labor women M.P.s follow the patterns set by the group as a whole. More Moderns were officers in the Labor Party, and fewer worked in the women's section. Far more Moderns were members of the Co-operative Party, a party organized in 1917 by the Co-operative Congress to promote socialism, and the Fabian Society, a group of Labor intellectuals. There was, however, a decline in the number of women M.P.s serving as union officers.

Among Conservative Moderns, 33% served as party officers, compared to 6% of the Pioneers. The percentage of M.P.s who served in the women's section declined from 18% to 9%.

The women's sections of the two major parties were organized to fulfill different functions. The Conservatives consider this a support group for candidates for Parliament. Lady Davidson, for example, was active in the women's section in the 1930s in order to organize campaign activity for her husband. In the Labor Party, on the other hand, the women's section is a political training organization, leading to fuller independent participation in other aspects of party activity. But, according to Lucy Middleton, all meetings of the Labor party women's section are held in the afternoon. Thus, few career women are able to use the women's section to gain a foothold in the political arena.[19] The women's section of both parties still supplies the real work force for all political campaigns, according to Lady Summerskill. A candidate should consider the strength of the women's section before deciding whether or not to run for office. Without a strong backing from that arm of the party, she feels that any candidate's chances for success are diminished.[20]

Conclusion

From the statistics presented in this chapter, we can draw a profile of the "typical" Labor Modern and her Conservative counterpart. Each differs significantly from her Pioneer predecessor.

The average Labor M.P. of the Modern era is forty-seven years old, a graduate of a state school and a university. She has a professional or business career and is also married and the mother of one or two children. Her husband comes from one of the professions. Her Pioneer ancestor came from a politically active family and was probably married to a man with a career in politics. The Pioneer won a seat in Parliament on her first attempt, but the Modern has had one unsuccessful campaign before winning. She has been active in the Labor party and was elected to an office in local government before winning national office.

The "typical" Conservative Modern is forty-three years old. Like her Pioneer predecessor, she attended a private school, but, unlike the Pioneer, she also attended a university and went on to a career in a profession or industry. She is likely to be single. If she is married, her husband works in industry and they have one or two children. She won on her first bid for Parliament, and before that held elected office on the local level. Although she has been an active party worker, she does not come from a politically active family. In this respect, she is very different from the "typical" Pioneer from her party, who was the wife or daughter of an M.P. and came from a family whose orientation was distinctly political.

5

A Comparison
of Successful and Unsuccessful
Women Candidates
for Parliament

Since the General Election of 1918, only ninety-four of the 568 women who have run for Parliament have been elected. What can we learn about the 474 women who were defeated? Were they distinctly different from those who won? Is there something in the background of the winners that gave them an edge? In order to compare the unsuccessful candidates with the winners, I have organized statistical material derived from their personal histories according to the pattern established in chapter 4 for the elected women.[1]

There were more candidates in Group II (Moderns) than in Group I (Pioneers), but there was a greater increase in the number of unsuccessful women candidates (156 to 318) than in the number of successful (39 to 55). As a result, the percentage of successful women candidates decreased from 20% in Group I to 15% in Group II. In examining these statistics in Group I along party lines, we find that the Conservatives had a greater percentage (41%) of successful women candidates than Labor (23%). Both major parties were stronger than the smaller parties (7%). The absolute numbers are shown in Table 1. In Group II Labor had more successful women candidates (32) than the Conservatives (21). Because Labor also had more women candidates standing, however, the Conservatives again had a higher percentage of successful candidates, 32%, as compared with 27% for the Labor Party and 1% for the smaller parties.

Successful vs. Unsuccessful Candidates:
A Comparison of Key Variables

The same variables that were considered for the women M.P.s in chapter 4 are analyzed in this chapter for the unsuccessful women can-

TABLE 1

*Number of Successful and Unsuccessful Women Candidates
for Parliament by Party: 1918-1970*

	Labor		Conservative		Other		Total	
Group I (1918-1935)								
	#	%	#	%	#	%	#	%
Successful	16	23	17	41	6	7	39	20
Unsuccessful	55	77	24	59	77	93	156	80
Total	*71*	*100*	*41*	*100*	*83*	*100*	*195*	*100*

	Labor		Conservative		Other		Total	
Group II (1945-1970)								
	#	%	#	%	#	%	#	%
Successful	32	27	21	32	2	1	55	15
Unsuccessful	85	73	66	68	167	99	318	85
Total	*117*	*100*	*87*	*100*	*169*	*100*	*373*	*100*

SOURCE: See Appendix

didates. The significance of the statistics for unsuccessful candidates in Group I is not as definitive in several areas as it is for the elected women M.P.s because of lack of biographical information. Many of the women who were not elected to Parliament made little impact on either the press or their parties. Hence, in many cases, it was difficult to obtain information about them, especially their ages, education, and husbands' occupations. In spite of the information gaps, however, a comparison of the unsuccessful candidates with those who were elected is valuable because the combined groups give us a better understanding of the women who have been active in national politics.

AGE

The age distribution of Group I women not elected when they made their first parliamentary bid is not really clear. Information is available for only twenty of the 156—too few to make any meaningful comparisons. Group II statistics are more nearly complete, wtih 243 observations available out of a total of 318 unsuccessful candidates. In Group II most women who were less than thirty years old were unsuccessful (one winner and thirty-eight losers). The only successful young woman represented one of the smaller parties. The older Labor (fifty and over) women made an impressive showing: approximately 50% of them won their seat (twelve out of twenty-five). In all the other age groups, the statistics show that the unsuccessful women candidates greatly outnumbered the successful, whether examined in terms of individual parties or combined party statistics.

TABLE 2

Age of Women Candidates at First Bid for Parliament

A. All Political Parties*

| | Group I (1918-1935) | | | | Group II (1945-1970) | | | |
| | Successful | | Unsuccessful | | Successful | | Unsuccessful | |
Age	#	%	#	%	#	%	#	%
20-29	2	6	8	40	1	2	38	16
30-39	13	39	7	35	20	38	72	30
40-49	12	36	2	10	16	30	83	34
50 & over	6	18	3	15	16	31	50	21
Total	33	99%	20	100%	53	101%	243	101%

*In Group I, information is missing for 6 successful and 136 unsuccessful candidates. In Group II, information is missing for 2 successful and 75 unsuccessful candidates.

B. Labor Party*

| | Group I (1918-1935) | | | | Group II (1945-1970) | | | |
| | Successful | | Unsuccessful | | Successful | | Unsuccessful | |
Age	#	%	#	%	#	%	#	%
20-29	1	8	3	38	—	—	8	11
30-39	5	42	3	38	11	37	28	37
40-49	2	17	1	12	7	23	27	36
50 & over	4	33	1	12	12	40	13	17
Total	12	100%	8	100%	30	100%	76	101%

*In Group I, information is missing for 4 successful and 47 unsuccessful candidates. In Group II, information is missing for 2 successful and 9 unsuccessful candidates.

C. Conservative Party*

| | Group I (1918-1935) | | | | Group II (1945-1970) | | | |
| | Successful | | Unsuccessful | | Successful | | Unsuccessful | |
Age	#	%	#	%	#	%	#	%
20-29	—	—	3	75	—	—	9	17
30-39	6	37	—	—	9	43	15	27
40-49	10	62	—	—	8	38	21	38
50 & over	—	—	1	25	4	19	10	18
Total	16	99%	4	100%	21	100%	55	100%

*In Group I, information is missing for 1 successful and 20 unsuccessful candidates. In Group II information is missing for no successful and 10 unsuccessful candidates.

SOURCE: See Appendix

Interviews with several unsuccessful candidates did not shed any light on these differences.[2] In general, the losers felt that every age had its disadvantages. A young career woman who entered politics was often criticized for being "too hard." If a woman was married and had children, she could not be a "good" wife and mother as well as a politician, according to the conventional wisdom. If a woman waited until her children were grown up before embarking on a political career then she had only a few years before she became "too old." The Labor women, Millie Miller and Judith Hart, were hopeful that these attitudes will change within a decade.[3]

EDUCATION

In the case of higher education, information sufficient for analysis is available only for the Group II women candidates. The data for the secondary school education for all unsuccessful candidates and for the higher education of unsuccessful Group I women do not allow a meaningful analysis. In Group II, the percent of successful women with a higher education (67%) was higher than for unsuccessful candidates

TABLE 3

*Higher Education of Candidates for Parliament
Successful and Unsuccessful
Group II (1945-1970)*

A. *All Political Parties*

Higher Education	Successful		Unsuccessful	
	#	%	#	%
Yes	37	67	173	54
Unknown	18	33	145	46
Total	55	100	318	100

B. *Labor Party*

Higher Education	Successful		Unsuccessful	
	#	%	#	%
Yes	21	66	61	72
Unknown	11	34	24	28
Total	32	100	85	100

C. *Conservative Party*

Higher Education	Successful		Unsuccessful	
	#	%	#	%
Yes	14	67	33	50
Unknown	7	33	33	50
Total	21	100	66	100

SOURCE: See Appendix

(54%). The Conservative women followed this general trend (67%-50%). For the Labor women, the same percentage (66%) of successful women had a higher education but a much higher (72%) percentage of unsuccessful women had received higher educations. This higher educational showing for Labor can perhaps be explained by the growth of the English training colleges. These teach skills (such as teaching and secretarial) and have been more popular with the Labor women from 6% up to 25% in Group II of the women attending colleges.

OCCUPATION

There are insufficient data to allow a valid comparison to be made of the employed and unemployed women in either group. However, the information available for the early years (Group I) shows that for women known to be employed, political and professions/business jobs were about even (42% and 47%). The remaining 11% are grouped under the term "other," which includes diverse occupations, such as student, gardener, farmer, and clerk. There is too little information to allow for a breakdown by party.

In the Modern period, Group II, the diverse occupations covered by "other" have grown, accounting for 39% of the total. There are still many women candidates whose careers are politically oriented, but many of these women are unsuccessful, so the percentage of winners in this occupational grouping has declined substantially. In Group II they accounted for only 15% of the successful women, compared to 37% of the unsuccessful candidates. These same relationships exist for both the Labor and Conservative parties.

FAMILY SITUATION

In examining the marital status of the women candidates, I have combined the statistics of the married women and the widows because the exact number of unsuccessful women who were widows is not available. In both Group I and Group II, approximately one-half of the unsuccessful candidates were single women. Single women represented a much lower percentage of successful candidates than the married women. These observations held in every case except for the successful Labor women in Group I. This group included such trade union activists as Margaret Bondfield and Ellen Wilkinson, as well as the dedicated social workers like Susan Lawrence and Dr. Marion Phillips.

The personal lives of candidates were given little coverage by any of the journals during their campaigns. It was seldom mentioned, for example, whether or not the candidates had children. I would suggest that the candidates themselves, particularly before World War II, tried

TABLE 4

Occupations of Women Candidates for Parliament

A. All Political Parties*

| | Group I (1918-1935) | | | | Group II (1945-1970) | | | |
| | Successful | | Unsuccessful | | Successful | | Unsuccessful | |
Occupation	#	%	#	%	#	%	#	%
Political	16	39	28	42	8	15	78	37
Prof/Business	12	29	31	47	35	66	52	25
Other	13	32	7	11	10	19	82	39
Total	*41*	*100%*	*66*	*100%*	*53*	*100%*	*212*	*101%*

*Information not available for 90 candidates in Group I and 106 in Group II.

B. Labor Party*

| | Group I (1918-1935) | | Group II (1945-1970) | | | |
| | | | Successful | | Unsuccessful | |
Occupation			#	%	#	%
Political			4	13	18	30
Prof/Business	Insufficient		21	66	9	15
Other	Data		7	22	32	54
Total			32	101%	59	99%

*Information not available for 27 candidates in Group I and 16 in Group II.

C. Conservative Party*

| | Group I (1918-1935) | | Group II (1945-1970) | | | |
| | | | Successful | | Unsuccessful | |
Occupation			#	%	#	%
Political			4	19	18	40
Prof/Business	Insufficient		13	62	10	22
Other	Data		4	19	17	38
Total			21	100%	45	100%

*Information not available for 17 candidates in Group I and 21 in Group II.

SOURCE: See Appendix

to avoid any charges of neglect by keeping their families in the background. In Group I, of seventy-nine married women who ran unsuccessful campaigns, only two were specifically mentioned as mothers. For Group II there was a little more information. Of the 180 unsuccessful married women, records are available on forty-four. In comparing the unsuccessful women with the women elected to Parliament, we find, as noted earlier, that a larger percentage of unsuccessful candidates were single. There was also a much smaller percentage of unsuccessful married women with children, but this is almost undoubtedly the result of

TABLE 5

Marital Status of Women Candidates for Parliament

A. All Political Parties

| Marital Status | Group I (1918-1935) | | | | Group II (1945-1970) | | | |
| | Successful | | Unsuccessful | | Successful | | Unsuccessful | |
	#	%	#	%	#	%	#	%
Married or								
Widowed	24	61	79	50	41	74	180	57
Single	15	38	77	49	14	26	138	43
Total	39	99%	156	99%	55	100%	318	100%

B. Labor Party

| Marital Status | Group I (1918-1935) | | | | Group II (1945-1970) | | | |
| | Successful | | Unsuccessful | | Successful | | Unsuccessful | |
	#	%	#	%	#	%	#	%
Married or								
Widowed	8	50	32	58	27	85	56	66
Single	8	50	23	42	5	16	29	34
Total	16	100%	55	100%	32	101%	85	100%

C. Conservative Party

| Marital Status | Group I (1918-1935) | | | | Group II (1945-1970) | | | |
| | Successful | | Unsuccessful | | Successful | | Unsuccessful | |
	#	%	#	%	#	%	#	%
Married or								
Widowed	12	71	9	38	13	62	36	55
Single	5	29	15	63	8	38	30	46
Total	17	100%	24	101%	21	100%	66	101%

SOURCE: See Appendix

missing information. Many more of the unsuccessful Group II Labor women and candidates from the smaller parties reported their children than did the Group II Conservative women.

POLITICAL EXPERIENCE

The largest number of unsuccessful women candidates from both Groups I and II ran only one time (64% and 71%, respectively), and the next largest percentage made a second unsuccessful attempt. These two patterns also hold for Groups I and II of both the Labor and Conservative parties. For those women who were elected, the largest percentages won on their first attempt (63% in Group I and 43% in Group II), and this pattern holds for Group I Conservatives and Labor

TABLE 6

Women Candidates with Children

A. All Political Parties*

| | Group I (1918-1935) | | | | Group II (1945-1970) | | | |
| | Successful | | Unsuccessful | | Successful | | Unsuccessful | |
Size of Family	#	%	#	%	#	%	#	%
Married or widowed, no children	6	19	77	49	7	16	136	43
Married or widowed, with 1-2 children	5	16	1	1	17	38	22	7
Married or widowed with 3-6 children	7	23	1	1	8	18	22	7
Single	13	41	77	49	13	29	138	43
Total	31	99%	156	100%	45	101%	318	100%

*Information is missing for 8 successful candidates in Group I, for 9 in Group II. For unsuccessful candidates, the statistics are approximate, based on best information available in political biographies.

B. Labor Party*

| | Group I (1918-1935) | | | | Group II (1945-1970) | | | |
| | Successful | | Unsuccessful | | Successful | | Unsuccessful | |
Size of Family	#	%	#	%	#	%	#	%
Married or widowed, no children	3	20	32	58	5	20	36	42
Married or widowed, with 1-2 children	3	20	0	—	11	44	9	11
Married or widowed, with 3-6 children	2	13	0	—	4	16	11	13
Single	7	47	23	42	5	20	29	34
Total	15	100%	55	100%	25	100%	85	100%

*For successful candidates, information is missing for 1 woman in Group I, 7 women in Group II. For unsuccessful candidates, statistics are approximate, based on best information available in political biographies.

TABLE 6 (*Continued*)

C. *Conservative Party**

Size of Family	Group I (1918-1935)				Group II (1945-1970)			
	Successful		Unsuccessful		Successful		Unsuccessful	
	#	%	#	%	#	%	#	%
Married or widowed, no children	3	21	9	37	3	15	34	52
Married or widowed, with 1-2 children	2	14	0	—	5	25	1	1
Married or widowed, with 3-6 children	5	36	0	—	4	20	1	1
Single	4	29	15	63	8	40	30	46
Total	14	100%	24	100%	20	100%	66	100%

*For successful candidates, information is missing for 3 women in Group I, 1 woman in Group II. For unsuccessful candidates, figures are approximate, based on best available information in political biographies.
SOURCE: *See* Appendix

and Group II Conservatives. Group II Labor women have a slightly different pattern, with 39% being successful on their second attempt compared with 36% on the first attempt. The above statistics, of course, reflect the characteristics of the women who won, and most of these won on their first or second attempt.

In order to determine the percentage which relate to the unsuccessful candidates, I subtracted the number of women who were successful and those women who chose not to run again from the total number of candidates. When the data are analyzed to reveal these results, they show that there are so many women who stood unsuccessfully only once or twice and then made no further attempts, that the total number who stood after having lost two attempts was very small. Thus, of those that did stand, three or more times (i.e., stood after two unsuccessful attempts), 22% of these candidates won.

Judith Hart expressed support for the idea of a candidate standing for a hopeless seat in order to gain political experience. She said many young women today who are not in a position to serve in Parliament at this time because of young children, are willing to accept the support of a hopeless constituency in order to prepare themselves for an eventual parliamentary career.[4]

In general, writers who have studied election trends believe that "the great majority of constituencies remain safe," even when there are "sharp jerks of partisan swings at elections."[5] Furthermore, "there is a

TABLE 7

Number of Attempts Made by Women Candidates
to Win a Seat in Parliament

A.   All Political Parties

Number of Campaigns	Group I (1918-1935)				Group II (1945-1970)			
	Successful		Unsuccessful		Successful		Unsuccessful	
	#	%	#	%	#	%	#	%
One	24	63	99	64	23	43	225	71
Two	7	18	37	24	16	30	56	18
Three	6	16	16	10	8	15	23	7
Four or More	1	3	4	3	7	13	14	4
Total	38	100%	156	101%	54	101%	318	100%

B.   Labor Party

Number of Campaigns	Group I (1918-1935)				Group II (1945-1970)			
	Successful		Unsuccessful		Successful		Unsuccessful	
	#	%	#	%	#	%	#	%
One	8	50	30	55	11	36	58	68
Two	3	19	18	33	12	39	15	18
Three	4	25	6	11	4	13	8	9
Four or more	1	6	1	2	4	13	4	5
Total	16	100%	55	101%	31	101%	85	100%

C.   Conservative Party

Number of Campaigns	Group I (1918-1935)				Group II (1945-1970)			
	Successful		Unsuccessful		Successful		Unsuccessful	
	#	%	#	%	#	%	#	%
One	13	81	16	67	10	48	43	65
Two	1	6	8	33	4	19	17	26
Three	2	13	0	—	4	19	4	6
Four or more	0	0	0	0	3	14	2	3
Total	16	100%	24	100%	21	100%	66	100%

For successful candidates, this refers to number of campaigns through first win. For unsuccessful candidates, the total number of campaigns is given.

SOURCE: See Appendix

'hard core' of party adherents who will vote Conservative, Liberal, or Labor as the case may be, irrespective of the issue of the moment, or their personal merits or demerits of the candidates."[6] This allegiance to party was evident in a remark made to a pollster during the General Election of 1951: "I would vote for a pig if my party put one up."[7]

In order to learn whether party allegiance is as important a factor when women are candidates, I examined the results of the elections immediately preceding the elections in which each of the 474 unsuc-

TABLE 8

*The Percentage of Candidates Who Were Successful
as a Function of How Many Times
They Had Run for Office*

A. *All Political Parties*

Times Ran	Group I (1918-1935)	Group II (1945-1970)
1-2	12%	8%
3 or more	22%	21%

B. *Labor Party*

Times Ran	Group I (1918-1935)	Group II (1945-1970)
1-2	11%	15%
3 or more	36%	29%

C. *Conservative Party*

Times Ran	Group I (1918-1935)	Group II (1945-1970)
1-2	27%	12%
3 or more	100%	39%

SOURCE: See Appendix

cessful women candidates took part. I did the same for the ninety-four successful women candidates. Such an analysis confirms the advantage of standing for a seat that was last held by one's party. A very high percentage of the successful women in Group I (38%) and in Group II (40%) were standing for a seat that had been won in the preceding election by their own party. On the other hand, only 4% of the unsuccessful women in Group I and 1% of the unsuccessful women in Group II had this advantage. Both Labor and Conservative women followed similar patterns, although the percentage was higher for the successful Conservative women candidates than for the Labor women (for Conservatives, 47% and 48% for Group I and II, respectively; for Labor, 31% and 37% for Group I and II, respectively). The Conservatives nominated a higher percentage of their women candidates for seats last held by the party than did Labor (23 out of 128—18%—for Conservatives, compared with 17 out of 188—9%—for Labor; calculated from data in Table 9).

The political activist, whether a suffragist or an elected political official, had an important advantage which distinguished the successful women candidates from the unsuccessful. The percentage of unsuccessful candidates who had been active in the suffragist movement or held elective public office was 25% in both Group I and Group II. A much higher percent of the successful women, 40% in Group I and 61% in Group II, had been suffragists or elected office holders. There was a substantial increase from the Group I period to the Group II period in the percent of women who had held elected office in local government from 12% to 24% for the unsuccessful and from 22% to 61% for the successful women. This pattern is the same for both the Labor and Conservative women.

A comparison of successful and unsuccessful women candidates reveals that a higher percentage of elected women came from politically active families than did unsuccessful women. This was especially true in Group I, where 41% of the successful women had husbands who had once been M.P.s, compared with only 4% of the unsuccessful women. A similarly one-sided situation existed for both the Labor and Conservative parties (38% versus 2% for Labor and 47% versus 4% for the Conservatives). Substantially fewer candidates had one parent who had once been an M.P., but again a greater portion of the successful candidates (15%) did have this relationship than did the unsuccessful (1%).

In Group II, political connections are less important. Eight percent of the successful candidates compared with only 3% of the unsuccessful were married to men who had once been an M.P., and similarly a higher percentage of successful women (6%) had one parent who had once been an M.P. For the unsuccessful candidates, this is true only for 1%. The results for both the Labor and Conservative parties during the Group II years are generally consistent with the results for "all parties." The exceptions are the Conservatives: not one of the twenty-one successful Conservative candidates was married to a man who had once been an M.P. In Group I, sixteen of the twenty-two women married to M.P.s themselves won seats. However, in Group II, only four of the fourteen women married to M.P.s won.

The present women candidates complain that too much emphasis is still placed on the family connections of potential candidates. Millie Miller, an unsuccessful Labor candidate, said the constituencies give preference to well-known names. Trixie Gardner, an unsuccessful Conservative candidate, told of her application for a constituency in which the Conservative member had recently died. She was interviewed and placed third on the constituency list (behind two men). However, the former member's wife decided to stand for the seat—to the dismay of the party, since she was an elderly cripple. To keep from hurting this woman, the party announced that its list was being cut after the two top names. Mrs. Gardner said a party never cuts its list before the top three names, but did so in this case in order not to have another woman's name appear on their list, i.e., not to offend the elderly widow. Consideration of Mrs. Gardner's fitness for office had no importance.

TABLE 9

Candidates Stood for Seat Previously
Held by Their Party

A. *All Political Parties*

| Seat Held Last by Party of Candidate | Group I (1918-1935) | | | | Group II (1945-1970) | | | |
| | Successful | | Unsuccessful | | Successful | | Unsuccessful | |
	#	%	#	%	#	%	#	%
Yes	15	38	6	4	22	40	4	1
No	24	62	150	96	33	60	314	99
Total	39	100%	156	100%	55	100%	318	100%

B. *Labor Party*

| Seat Held Last by Party of Candidate | Group I (1918-1935) | | | | Group II (1945-1970) | | | |
| | Successful | | Unsuccessful | | Successful | | Unsuccessful | |
	#	%	#	%	#	%	#	%
Yes	5	31	0	0	12	37	0	0
No	11	69	55	100	20	63	85	100
Total	16	100%	55	100%	32	100%	85	100%

C. *Conservative Party*

| Seat Held Last by Party of Candidate | Group I (1918-1935) | | | | Group II (1945-1970) | | | |
| | Successful | | Unsuccessful | | Successful | | Unsuccessful | |
	#	%	#	%	#	%	#	%
Yes	8	47	3	12	10	48	2	3
No	9	53	21	88	11	52	64	97
Total	17	100%	24	100%	21	100%	66	100%

SOURCE: See Appendix

Party experience also seems to have been an important qualification distinguishing the successful from the unsuccessful women candidates. In Group I, 91% of the successful candidates had party experience, compared with only 26% of the unsuccessful candidates. Both the Labor and Conservative parties have similar patterns.

Party experience is still important in Group II, with 92% of the successful women from "all parties" having worked in their parties. Successful candidates in both major parties also recorded a similar high percentage of work within their parties. However, the percentage of unsuccessful women with party experience climbed to 56% for "all parties" and 68% for Conservatives. The Labor women who were successful (94%) were very active in their party, but only 26% of the unsuccessful candidates recorded party work.

TABLE 10

Number of Women Candidates for Parliament
Previously Active in Suffragist Movement
or Elected to Public Office

A. All Political Parties

	Group I (1918-1935)				Group II (1945-1970)			
	Successful		Unsuccessful		Successful		Unsuccessful	
Elected Office	#	%	#	%	#	%	#	%
Local Govt.	11	22	23	15	34	61	78	25
Suffragist	9	18	15	10	0	—	0	—
No	29	59	118	76	22	39	240	75
Total	49	99%	156	101%	56	100%	318	100%

B. Labor Party

	Group I (1918-1935)				Group II (1945-1970)			
	Successful		Unsuccessful		Successful		Unsuccessful	
Elected Office	#	%	#	%	#	%	#	%
Local Govt.	6	26	13	24	20	63	28	33
Suffragist	7	31	6	11	0	—	0	—
No	10	44	36	65	12	37	57	67
Total	23	101%	55	100%	32	100%	85	100%

C. Conservative Party

	Group I (1918-1935)				Group II (1945-1970)			
	Successful		Unsuccessful		Successful		Unsuccessful	
Elected Office	#	%	#	%	#	%	#	%
Local Govt.	2	11	3	13	14	64	29	44
Suffragist	1	6	0	—	0	—	0	—
No	15	83	21	87	8	36	37	56
Total	18	100%	24	100%	22	100%	66	100%

SOURCE: See Appendix

Interviews with Three Unsuccessful
Women Candidates

A. AN UNSUCCESSFUL LABOR CANDIDATE

Although Millie Miller made her first parliamentary stand in the British General Election of 1974, she had been interested in standing for Parliament since the early part of the 1960s but couldn't find a constituency that would accept her as a candidate. She explained that "women were out of fashion." So she turned her attention to local government and was elected to serve as mayor of Stoke Newington from 1957 until 1958. She was also mayor of Camden (1967-68), as well as leader of the Camden Council (1971-73).

TABLE 11

Political Activity of Families of
Women Candidates for Parliament

A. All Political Parties*

Husband	Group I (1918-1935)				Group II (1945-1970)			
an M.P.	Successful		Unsuccessful		Successful		Unsuccessful	
	#	%	#	%	#	%	#	%
Yes	16	41	6	4	4	8	10	3
No	23	59	150	96	51	93	308	97
Total	39	100%	156	100%	55	101%	318	100%
Parent an M.P.								
Yes	6	15	2	1	3	6	3	1
No	33	85	154	99	52	94	315	99
Total	39	100%	156	100%	55	100%	318	100%

*One successful Group II candidate, Shirley Summerskill, was the daughter of a successful Group I candidate, Edith, Lady Summerskill. All other M.P. parents were fathers.

B. Labor Party*

Husband	Group I (1918-1935)				Group II (1945-1970)			
an M.P.	Successful		Unsuccessful		Successful		Unsuccessful	
	#	%	#	%	#	%	#	%
Yes	6	38	1	2	4	12	3	4
No	10	63	54	98	28	88	82	97
Total	16	101%	55	100%	32	100%	85	101%
Parent an M.P.								
Yes	1	6	0	—	2	6	0	—
No	15	94	55	100	30	94	85	100
Total	16	100%	55	100%	32	100%	85	100%

*One successful Group II candidate, Shirley Summerskill, was the daughter of a successful Group I candidate, Edith, Lady Summerskill. All other M.P. parents were fathers.

C. Conservative Party

Husband	Group I (1918-1935)				Group II (1945-1970)			
an M.P.	Successful		Unsuccessful		Successful		Unsuccessful	
	#	%	#	%	#	%	#	%
Yes	8	47	1	4	0	—	3	5
No	9	53	23	96	21	100	63	96
Total	17	100%	24	100%	21	100%	66	101%
Parent an M.P.								
Yes	2	12	2	8	2	10	1	2
No	15	88	22	92	19	90	65	99
Total	17	100%	24	100%	21	100%	66	101%

SOURCE: See Appendix

TABLE 12

*Political Party Experience of Women Candidates
for Parliament*

A.   *All Political Parties*

Party	Group I (1918-1935)				Group II (1945-1970)			
	Successful		Unsuccessful		Successful		Unsuccessful	
Experience	#	%	#	%	#	%	#	%
Worker	20	38	18	12	19	21	43	14
Officer	4	8	11	7	19	21	81	25
Women's Section	10	19	7	4	7	8	31	10
Nat. Exec. Bd.	7	13	3	2	12	13	22	7
Other	7	13	—	—	26	29	—	—
Subtotal	*48*	*91*	*39*	*25*	*83*	*92*	*177*	*56*
None	5	10	117	75	7	8	141	44
Total	*53*	*101%*	*156*	*100%*	*90*	*100%*	*318*	*100%*

B.   *Labor Party*

Party	Group I (1918-1935)				Group II (1945-1970)			
	Successful		Unsuccessful		Successful		Unsuccessful	
Experience	#	%	#	%	#	%	#	%
Worker	8	29	11	20	8	15	8	9
Officer	3	11	2	4	7	13	11	13
Women's Section	4	14	2	4	4	7	2	2
Nat. Exec. Bd.	6	22	0	—	9	17	2	2
Other	6*	22	—	—	23	42	—	—
Subtotal	*27*	*98*	*15*	*28*	*51*	*94*	*23*	*26*
None	1	2	40	73	3	6	62	73
Total	*28*	*100%*	*55*	*101%*	*54*	*100%*	*85*	*99%*

*In Group I, two union officers, one member of Co-op Party, three members
of Fabian Society. In Group II, one union officer, 14 members of Co-op Party,
8 members of Fabian Society.

C.   *Conservative Party*

Party	Group I (1918-1935)				Group II (1945-1970)			
	Successful		Unsuccessful		Successful		Unsuccessful	
Experience	#	%	#	%	#	%	#	%
Worker	9	53	1	4	10	30	11	17
Officer	1	6	1	4	11	33	21	32
Women's Section	3	18	2	8	3	9	9	14
Nat. Exec. Bd.	1	6	0	—	2	6	3	5
Other	1	6	—	—	3	9	—	—
Subtotal	*15*	*89*	*4*	*16*	*29*	*87*	*44*	*68*
None	2	12	20	83	4	12	22	33
Total	*17*	*101%*	*24*	*99%*	*33*	*99%*	*66*	*101%*

SOURCE: See Appendix

Mrs. Miller was educated in a small girls' school and did not receive a college education. She has worked as a social worker. She is married and has two grown children. She lives in London and has long been an active worker in the Labor Party.

The seat (Redbridge Ilford North) that she contested had been held by a Conservative man for twenty years. She was planning to stand for this same seat in the October 1974 election. Her expectations were high because in the February election she had been defeated by only two hundred votes. The Labor Party was very enthusiastic about her chances that October but she was again unsuccessful.

Mrs. Miller feels that the climate of opinion is changing in favor of giving women a more nearly equal opportunity. This attitude is reflected in party encouragement to women to stand for Parliament and in constituency acceptance of women's candidacy. The average Labor woman candidate, however, faces two problems in securing safe seats: the importance of family connections and union influence. In assessing a candidate's chances to be nominated by any constituency, she said a Trade Union sponsored candidate would be a first choice, a male lawyer would be next, and the remaining prospective men and women candidates would be viewed impartially, unless one of these candidates was a relative of a Labor stalwart. The Labor women within a constituency are often reluctant to support a woman candidate because they recognize the problems faced by women candidates, family pressures, and the uphill battle to win political acceptance. Once selected, however, a woman candidate receives full support from the women within the constituency.

The short list that the Labor Party considered in Mrs. Miller's constituency was composed of four names: her own, another woman's, and two men's. She feels that women candidates are generally better qualified than their male counterparts and points out that her present constituency told her that had she chosen not to accept their invitation to stand, they would have selected the second woman, a personal friend of hers.

B. An Unsuccessful Conservative Candidate

Trixie Gardner was born in Australia. She and her husband emigrated to London in 1956. They are both dentists and share a joint office in London. Their three children were born in Britain and range in age from eight to fourteen. European *au pair* girls help Mrs. Gardner manage her home.

Mrs. Gardner comes from a politically active family. Her father was Minister for Health and Deputy Premier of New South Wales, and her uncle was Premier of New South Wales. When she arrived in London, she contacted the Conservative Party and offered her services. She was given the job of cooking in a home for the elderly. She also joined the local women's section of the Conservative Party. She noted that this group was composed of elderly women who made the organization a closed club, exciting no real effort to attract young women. She became president of the club and tried to encourage active participation in party affairs but made few lasting changes.

She asked the Central party office in 1966 to put her name on their list of prospective candidates but was advised to get local government experience first. She was elected to the Westminster Council for four years, then approached the party again. She was told that the candidates list was closed. Furious, she forced the issue and was finally accepted but was given a hopeless seat (Blackburn) to fight. After this experience, she decided not to accept another constituency that was hopeless. However, she did accept a constituency (Cornwall North) in the February 1974 General Election because the constituency asked for her by name. Again she went down to defeat. She is determined to secure a reasonably safe seat before making another parliamentary effort but has not yet been offered one. Although she is very enthusiastic about a parliamentary career, she fears that, because she is forty-seven years old, she will soon be too old for another parliamentary effort.

In order to secure a reasonably safe constituency, Mrs. Gardner believes that women must be clearly better qualified than male candidates. In one case known to her, the local Conservative agent simply discarded the names of any women sent to his constituency before drawing up a prospective candidates list. She stated, too, that the constituencies' committees always give preference to well-known names. Since the General Election in 1970, the Central Office has lost power over the constituencies, who are now tending to select locally known candidates, but Mrs. Gardner does not see this as a continuing trend, only a temporary effect of weak leadership.

C. An Unsuccessful Liberal Candidate

Margaret Winfield is a dedicated Liberal who has stood for Parliament four times. She believes that campaigning is a good experience and should be undertaken at least once before securing a safe seat. Although she was offered a constituency for the October 1974 election, she did not plan to stand, because her husband, an engineer, had taken early retirement.

Mrs. Winfield has four grown children. One of her sons is studying law and will enter politics eventually after first gaining legal experience.

She feels that the Liberal Party encourages women to stand but can offer few safe seats, because the Party itself is weak in comparison to the other major parties. She did face discrimination within her first constituency of Wokingham. She was asked to stand for the General

Election in 1964, knowing that the fight was hopeless. She fought the contest with great determination and succeeded in raising the Liberal vote considerably. She was asked to stand again for the constituency in the 1966 election but then heard that her proposed candidacy was causing dissension within the Liberal ranks. The very scope of the Liberal success in Wokingham after her 1964 campaign had convinced some of the Liberal members of the constituency that if they had been represented by a male candidate they might have won. The leader of the rebels was a local politician, a man, for whom she had successfully campaigned. She withdrew her name and a man was subsequently chosen, only to have the Liberal strength in the constituency slide back to its pre-1964 status.

An active worker within the Liberal Party, Mrs. Winfield is presently in a two-way contest for the presidency of the Liberal Party.

Conclusion

A study of the key variables shows that there is a difference between successful and unsuccessful women candidates for Parliament. In examining individual cases these differences aren't striking, but the cumulative information shows clearly that family connections have been a crucial factor, as well as political and party experience. These three factors all help to make the candidate known to her party, constituency, and the electorate and often give her an edge over other potential candidates with less exposure and experience.

A young single woman is at the greatest disadvantage with the electorate. In both parties for both Pioneers and Moderns, married women have been more successful, except for the Labor Pioneer women. This deviation can be explained by the activity of Labor's outstanding mature career women. In only a few cases has a young unmarried woman been successful.

Success in many cases depends upon relentless determination, despite repeated defeats. Many unsuccessful women candidates have dropped out after repeated failures at the polls. But if a woman can sustain her enthusiasm for hard work, her eventual chance of success increases greatly.

Although the Conservatives have had fewer women M.P.s they had had a higher percentage of successful women in both Groups than the Labor Party. One can explain the success of the Conservative women in Group I by the large percentage (47%) who took their husbands' seats, but this was not true in Group II (0%). The statistics show also that in Group II the Conservatives gave almost half (48%) of their women candidates seats to contest that had been held previously by the Conservative Party. The Labor Party does field a higher number of candidates but allocates fewer safe seats to them. The importance of running for a seat that has been previously held by one's party cannot be overstated.

Millie Miller has worked in the Labor Party and has held elective office. Despite these advantages, she feels the effects of the party's basic allegiance to male candidates. Because of the success she made in her last election effort, however, her chances are considered very promising. On the other hand, Trixie Gardner, has not been a worker in the Conservative Central Office, working more on the periphery of the party. She has been an active and successful member of local government. She, too, finds it difficult to overcome the party's preference for male candidates. She did not have a constituency for the October 1974 election because she refused to accept a constituency that would be hopeless. The Liberal Party, of course, does not now have many safe seats. Margaret Winfield has been an active worker in the Liberal Party and is currently a Justice of the Peace. With the Liberal Party's upswing in popularity, she feels that she would have a good chance of winning a seat if she were younger.

Perhaps the most striking fact about all three women is their devotion to politics despite the lack of party support. Even when it is given, such support is often grudgingly bestowed. Each woman must work to overcome prejudice almost as if it were the beginning of the struggle, rather than fifty long years since women were given the right to stand for election.

6

A Comparison of the Men and Women Elected to Parliament in the General Elections of 1929, 1945, and 1970

In this chapter, I compare the men and women who won seats in Parliament in the general elections of 1929, 1945, and 1970. The first two elections were milestones in British history. The year 1929 saw the first general election in which all women of twenty-one years and over were allowed to vote. The election of 1945 was the first held since England emerged from the devastation of World War II and the first in ten years. (For the same reasons, it is the year chosen to separate the Pioneers and Moderns among women M.P.s, as explained in chapter 2.) The 1970 election was included in this study because it was the most recent in Parliamentary history at the time this research began.

The General Election of 1929

As the parties prepared for the election of 1929, the Conservatives, in power since 1924, were faced with challenges from the still active Liberal Party and a steadily growing Labor Party. It was a significant year for several reasons. This would prove to be the last election in which a majority of the seats were contested by three candidates. The electorate, moreover, had been enlarged by 16.5% with the addition of the "flapper vote."[1] The extension of the franchise to adult women had been supported wholeheartedly by the Labor Party for many years. In October 1924, Arthur Henderson, a Labor M.P., had predicted that "unless the Labour Government is returned to office, there is no chance of the women getting votes on the same terms as men."[2] Now that women had the right to vote, would they support Labor at the polls? This untested group might overturn traditional voting patterns. All parties set out to court the new voters, through new campaign strategies.[3] Fears that the political process would be undermined by the presence of women proved to be groundless, just as they had in the general election of 1918, when women over thirty years of age were first allowed to vote. Now as then, "there was no evidence that women had behaved any differently from men."[4]

The major issue in 1929 was unemployment. The Conservatives, led by Stanley Baldwin, had had five years to solve the problem but had failed. Now they had no new solutions to offer but based their campaign on a slogan of "Safety First." This slogan was directed toward the British electorate fears that had been aroused by the General Strike of 1926. The failure of the Strike, however, had actually raised the appeal of the Labor Party. The party, under Ramsay MacDonald's leadership, was now considered a better vehicle than the unions to implement change. The influence of the more extreme elements of the party was reduced so that a moderate platform was offered to the electorate. The contest was between the Conservative and Labor parties, even though the Liberals, under David Lloyd George's leadership, offered the most comprehensive proposals for the British problems. Lloyd George's proposals, however, were viewed with skepticism by the electorate, because he had also promised a better world after World War I.

There was a large group of candidates in 1929: 596 Conservatives (10 women), 571 Labor (30 women), 514 Liberals (25 women), and 47 minor parties (3 women). On May 30, 1929, the voters decided that they were ready for a change: Labor won, but not with a majority. The Labor Party acquired only 288 seats. The Conservatives, with 260 seats, and the Liberals, with a meager 59, could form a coalition and upset Labor plans. Thus, although Ramsay MacDonald was asked to form a new government, he and his party were not to be allowed to implement their platform.

What types of members had been elected? In all there were 601 men and 13 women. (Fifty percent of the women candidates and 51% of the male candidates had been elected.) Among the women M.P.s were three Conservatives, nine Labor, one Liberal, and one Independent. The average age of the women (46.5) was lower than the average age of the men (50.5). In fact, 23% of the women were under thirty-six. The Labor Party presented the extremes in age, with the oldest M.P., sixty-eight-year-old Dr. Ethel Bentham, and the youngest, twenty-five-year-old Jennie Lee.[5]

Secondary education statistics for successful candidates in 1929 are not fully recorded. In one published chart an analyst estimated that 53% of the M.P.s had attended private schools and 56% public schools.[6] This information is unavailable for nine of the fourteen women M.P.s. Two of the remaining five women were educated privately (Cynthia, Lady Mosley, a Labor member, and Katharine, Duchess of Atholl, a

Conservative), and three attended public schools (Jennie Lee, Ellen Wilkinson, and Margaret Bondfield. All three were Labor members).

TABLE 1-A

Age in Year of Election
Comparison of Women and Men M.P.s
All Parties, 1929

Age	Women		Men	
	Number	Percent	Number	Percent
Below 36	3	23	39	6.5
36-50	4	31	196	32.5
51-64	5	38	187	31
Over 64	1	8	50	8
Unknown	0	0	129	21.5
Total	*13*	*100*	*601*	*99.5*

SOURCE: See Appendix

The percentage of male M.P.s with British college or university training (42%), together with the one percent educated abroad, equals the percentage educated in private schools (43%). A higher percentage of women M.P.s (64%) had received British university training and an additional 7% had been educated abroad. In this period the secondary (private) school that male candidates attended was noted by the candidates and given at least equal importance as their university or college. This was not the case for women candidates.[7]

Turning to occupations, we find that the largest group of men were engaged in the professions (48%), whereas the largest number of women were concentrated in political activities (43%). Only 21% of the women held professional positions; only 15% of the men held political jobs. (See chapter 4 for definitions of "professional" and "political" occupations.) A large group of male M.P.s (24%) did not list an occupation, but published charts estimated that 37% of those who listed no occupations were in fact manual workers. Among women M.P.s, 36% were listed as "not employed." This category is made up of married women who held no salaried job outside the home.

A lack of political experience on the local level did not seem to be a handicap for parliamentary candidates. Of the M.P.s elected in 1929, 70% of the men and 57% of the women had not been elected to any previous political office. Party breakdowns are revealing in this regard. None of the Conservative women, and twice as many Labor as Conservative men, had been elected to local government office before winning seats in Parliament in 1929.

TABLE 2-A

Education of Women and Men M.P.s
*All Parties, 1929**

	Women†		Men	
Age	Number	Percent	Number	Percent
University	9	64	256	42.5
Abroad	1	7	2	.3
None/unknown	4	28	343	57
Total	*14*	*99*	*601*	*99.8*

---

*The statistics for the male candidates at school level have been taken from published works. Ross, *Parliamentary Representation*, p. 4. The information on the women: see chapter 4.
†Statistics for one Conservative woman unknown.

SOURCE: See Appendix

TABLE 3-A

Occupation in Year of Election
Comparison of Women and Men M.P.s
All Parties, 1929

	Women		Men	
Occupation	Number	Percent	Number	Percent
Political†	6	43	88	14.6
Professional**	3	21	286	47.5
Manual workers	0	0	81	13
Not employed/ unknown	5	36	146*	24
Total	*14*	*100*	*601*	*99.1*

---

*Ross, *Parliamentary Representation*, p. 61, lists these 146 candidates as manual workers but they did not so identify themselves in *Dod's Parliamentary Companion*.
†Elected office holders, union organizers, and civil servants.
**Professions include law, teaching, journalism, medicine, and theater. Positions in business are at the management level.

SOURCE: See Appendix

Among successful male candidates, work in their political parties did not seem a significant factor in winning. Only 16% of the men were readily identified as party workers. On the other hand, 93% of the women had worked for their parties. This strong showing by the women in the Pioneer group was noted in chapter 4 and was attributed to their support of their husbands' careers as well as their own ambitions. If we consider the number of times an M.P. ran for election before his or her first success, we find similar percentages for the men and women M.P.s. Fifty-nine percent of the men and 50% of the women won on their first attempt. A large percentage (36% of the women, 21% of the men) won on their second attempts. Thereafter, there is a sharp decline in percentages. It appears that for candidates in this group, first and second campaigns were crucial.

When the winning party forms a new government, do its leaders appoint women M.P.s to important posts? There seems little doubt that the Labor Party has given its women members wider opportunities. In its first government in 1923, the Labor Party appointed Margaret Bondfield to the post of Parliamentary Secretary to the Ministry of Labor, and Susan Lawrence to the post of Parliamentary Private Secretary to the President of the Board of Education. Evidently embarrassed by their previous record, the Conservatives appointed the Duchess of Atholl to the post of Parliamentary Secretary to the Board of Education when they returned to power in 1924. (See chapter 1.) In the 1929 government, Labor named Margaret Bondfield as Minister of Labor. She

TABLE 4-A

Experience in Local Government
Comparison of Women and Men M.P.s
All Parties, 1929

	Women		Men	
	Number	Percent	Number	Percent
Elected office	6	43	133	22
No elected office	8	57	421	70
Unknown	0	0	47	7.8
Total	*14*	*100*	*601*	*99.8*

SOURCE: See Appendix

TABLE 5-A

Party Workers
Comparison of Women and Men M.P.s
All Parties, 1929

	Women		Men	
	Number	Percent	Number	Percent
Party worker	13	93	95	15.7
Not Party worker	1	7	469	77.9
Unknown	0	0	37	6.1
Total	*14*	*100*	*601*	*99.7*

SOURCE: See Appendix

TABLE 6-A

Number of Campaigns Before First Election to Parliament
Comparisons of Women and Men M.P.s
All Parties, 1929

No. of Previous	Women		Men	
Campaigns	Number	Percent	Number	Percent
0	7	50	358	59.5
1	5	36	125	20.7
2	1	7	56	9
3	1	7	34	5.6
4	0	0	11	1.8
5	0	0	4	.6
6	0	0	0	0
7	0	0	0	0
Unknown	0	0	13	2
Total	*14*	*100*	*601*	*99.2*

SOURCE: See Appendix

thus became the first woman Cabinet Minister.[8] Susan Lawrence was appointed Parliamentary Secretary to the Ministry of Health. Two other women became Parliamentary Private Secretaries: Mary Agnes Hamilton was appointed by C. R. Attlee, Chancellor of the Duchy of Lancaster, and Ellen Wilkinson was appointed by Susan Lawrence.

The General Election of 1945

The general election of 1945 was held during the unsettled aftermath of World War II. Britain had been governed since 1940 by a coalition government headed by Winston Churchill. When the war in Europe ended, the coalition began to disintegrate. A general election was called for July 1945. The candidates and their parties were faced with the herculean task of identifying their supporters and organizing campaigns that would be relevant to the changing times. Traditional party ties had been disrupted by the uprooting of a large segment of the British population during the war years. Furthermore, the party machinery was rusty. As evidence that the major parties had been weakened, Independent candidates defeated more Labor and Conservative candidates than they had previously done in all general elections since 1918.[9]

The British people in 1945 were facing many domestic and international problems. The long-standing problems of the British underprivileged had been widely recognized during the war years as the English classes were brought into closer proximity as a result of the shifting of large segments of the population from the cities to escape the bombing, as well as through service in the defense organizations. On the international scene, Britain had to set a policy for its future relationship with India and Russia. In all areas, the Labor Party, led by Clement Attlee, offered new approaches to both the domestic and international issues. The Conservatives, on the other hand, campaigned on the wartime reputation of Winston Churchill. They had no new suggestion for domestic affairs and were burdened by their traditionally negative reaction to improved relations with both India and Russia.

Voters chose from among 1,683 candidates—one of the largest groups ever to stand.[10] Labor fielded 604 candidates (41 women), the Conservatives 573 (14 women), the Liberals 307 (20 women), and the remaining parties a total of 196 (12 women). Many of the candidates were still serving in the armed services.

The voters turned Churchill out and gave Labor its first clear victory with 393 seats. The Conservatives, with 189, had only twice before been so badly defeated (1832 and 1906). The Liberals won 12 seats and the remaining parties 46. With such a majority, Labor was at last free to move forward with its own programs.

A total of 616 men and 24 women took their seats in the House of Commons. (Twenty-five percent of all women candidates and 38% of all male candidates won.) Twenty-one of the women were from the Labor Party. There was one Conservative woman (Joan, Lady Davidson), one Liberal (Megan Lloyd George), and one Independent (Eleanor Rathbone). The average age of women M.P.s was higher than in any election before or since—fifty. For the men, the average age was slightly lower—forty-six.[11] In 1929, the situation had been the opposite, but after World War II all parties were seeking new talent and younger men.[12] And, with traditional careers uprooted, more men were willing to enter the political arena. The women who were elected to Parliament, on the other hand, were all experienced party workers. Many had already held local elective offices. Thirty-five of the 87 women candidates had sought election to Parliament before 1945. Mrs. Lucy Middleton was typical. Like many other women, she had been waiting a long time for recognition from her party.

Because twenty-one of the women M.P.s were from the Labor Party, it is not surprising to find that most were educated in state schools. Mrs. Florence Paton, who was educated by a tutor, was the one Labor exception. Each of the Conservative, Liberal, and Independent women M.P.s had received private school educations. Information was available for only 75% of the male members, but the percentage remained consistent with the 1929 results, whereby 44% of the male members received a private education and 56% were educated in state schools.[13]

The educational background of male M.P.s follows the same pattern at the university level. Only one-half had any advanced education. Among women M.P.s, 8% had been educated abroad, and 58% had attended

TABLE 1-B

Age in Year of Election
Comparison of Women and Men M.P.s
All Parties, 1945

Age	Women Number	Percent	Men Number	Percent
Below 36	2	8	15	2.4
36-50	7	29.1	160	25.9
51-64	10	41.6	206	33.4
Over 64	2	8.3	138	22.3
Unknown	3	12	97	15.7
Total	*24*	*99.0*	*616*	*99.7*

SOURCE: See Appendix

British universities and colleges. Only 33% had received no higher education.

The occupations of the men and women M.P.s follow similar patterns. Forty-two percent of the men and 50% of the women held professional positions. In the political category, 33% of the women and 35% of the men were represented. Seventeen percent of the women were not employed before entering Parliament, i.e., were married women who had not held salaried positions. In the breakdown among the professions, the men and women are similar. More Labor members worked in journalism, teaching, and medicine; more Conservatives were represented in business and law.

Members of Parliament elected in 1945 did not have a great deal of local political experience, but, as in 1929, the women (46%) were better prepared than the men (34%). Repeating the 1929 pattern, more than five times as many Labor M.P.s had served in local office as Conservatives.

Nearly all women M.P.s (96%) were party workers, but this was true for only 15% of the men. This indicates that women were continuing to use party activity to gain access to political office, whereas male candidates could depend on accomplishments in other areas.

The majority of the men (67%) won their seats on the first attempt. More women were successful in their second contest (42%) than in their first (29%).

Labor women were appointed to several government offices in the new Labor government. Ellen Wilkinson became Minister of Education. Two women were named Parliamentary Secretaries: Edith Summerskill to the Ministry of Food, and Jennie Adamson to the Ministry of Pensions. Although many more women were now in important posts, these were limited to fields that were traditionally considered of interest to women.

TABLE 2-B

Education of Women and Men M.P.s
All Parties, 1945*

Education	Women		Men	
	Number	Percent	Number	Percent
University	14	58	302	49
Abroad	2	8	24	3
None/unknown	8†	33	290	48
Total	24	99	616	100

*Statistics on school level for the men found in McCallum. See chapter 4 for the women.
†Statistics unknown for two women.

SOURCE: See Appendix

TABLE 3-B

Occupation in Year of Election
Comparison of Women and Men M.P.s
All Parties, 1945

Occupation	Women		Men	
	Number	Percent	Number	Percent
Political*	8	33	215	34.8
Professional†	12	50	258	41.8
Manual Worker	0	0	54	8.7
Not employed	4	17	0	0
Unknown	0	0	89	14
Total	24	100	616	99.3

*Elected office holders, union organizers, and civil servants.
†Professions include law, teaching, journalism, medicine, and theater. Positions in business are at the management level.

SOURCE: See Appendix

TABLE 4-B

Experience in Local Government
Comparison of Women and Men M.P.s
All Parties, 1945

	Women		Men	
	Number	Percent	Number	Percent
Elected office	11	46	207	33.5
No elected office	13	54	386	62.6
Unknown	0	0	23	3.7
Total	24	100	616	99.8

SOURCE: See Appendix

TABLE 5-B

Party Workers
Comparison of Women and Men M.P.s
All Parties, 1945

	Women		Men	
	Number	Percent	Number	Percent
Party worker	23	96	89	14.7
Not a party worker	1	4	504	83
Unknown	0	0	23	1.8
Total	*24*	*100*	*616*	*99.5*

SOURCE: See Appendix

TABLE 6-B

Number of Campaigns
Before First Election to Parliament
Comparison of Women and Men M.P.s
All Parties, 1945

Number of Previous	Women		Men	
Campaigns	Number	Percent	Number	Percent
0	7	29	413	67
1	10	42	110	17.8
2	4	17	47	7.6
3	2	8	18	2.9
4	1	4	10	1.6
5	0	0	2	.3
6	0	0	0	0
7	0	0	1	.2
Unknown	0	0	15	2.4
Total	*24*	*100*	*616*	*99.8*

SOURCE: See Appendix

The General Election of 1970

The general election of 1970 was called by Harold Wilson in June rather than the autumn because of Labor's apparent strength with the electorate. Labor had been in power since 1964 and had never felt more secure. The major issues of the campaign were economic. Thus, the timing of the general election was important. "The result of the election would depend on the timing of the trade cycle and the public opinion cycle which was largely dependent on it."[14] In April, when Wilson announced the election, the economy was strong and there was a heavy trade surplus. But balance-of-payment problems were being predicted by Conservatives. The public opinion polls that had given the Conservatives a 19% edge in July, 1969, showed Labor in the lead by 7.5% in May, 1970. The efforts of the Liberals, under the leadership of Jeremy Thorpe, aroused little public interest. In general, Liberals were taking their few votes from both sides equally and were not considered a major threat by either Labor or Conservative.

The two major parties conducted very different types of campaigns. The Conservatives were not wildly enthusiastic about their new leader, Edward Heath. He was inexperienced and bland. Heath's personal appearances were carefully staged. Nevertheless, he did not seem to be reaching the voters. The Conservative Party continued to slide in the opinion polls. The Labor candidate, on the other hand, followed Wilson's lead in not giving specific details of party policies. They spoke in generalities, hoping to maintain their popularity. Wilson took his campaign to the people, going on walking tours through the cities. The success of this type of campaigning forced Heath to change his careful style. He began to make more "spontaneous" appearances. But the polls showed Labor in the lead right up to voting day.

There were 1,837 candidates standing for Parliament in the 1970 general election. Labor fielded 624 candidates (29 women), the Conservatives 628 (26 women), and the remaining parties 242 (21 women). More candidates were running for the first time in this election than in any since 1945.[15]

On June 18, 1970, the Conservatives won the general election—a genuine upset. They were given a working majority of 30. The economic difficulties that the Conservatives had been predicting came alive to the voters on June 15, when the monthly trade figures from May showed a deficit for the first time in nine months. There were not great changes in voting patterns, but the uncommitted voter tended to favor the Conservatives as the "lesser of two evils."[16] The Conservatives won 330 seats, Labor 287, the Liberals 6, and other parties 6. The swing cost many well-known Labor politicians their seats. Jennie Lee lost her safe seat (Cannock), as did Gyneth and John Dunwoody, the only married couple then serving as M.P.s. (They were the sixth couple to serve in the Commons together.)

A total of 604 men and 26 women took their seats in the new Parliament. (Twenty-six percent of all women candidates and 34% of all men candidates had been elected.) Among the women M.P.s, there were 15 Conservative, 10 Labor, and one Independent Unity members. At 23, Bernadette Devlin (Independent Unity) was the youngest M.P. Labor had one man who was in his twenites. But this was the first election in which there were no Conservative M.P.s under thirty. The average age of the M.P.s was forty-nine for the women and forty-nine for the men. This increased age is a reflection of parliamentary experi-

ence, because 76% of the M.P.s elected in 1970 had served in the preceding government.

Information about schooling for M.P.s elected in 1970 is more extensive, with 79% recorded, than the earlier elections. Among the men,
60% attended state schools and 40% attended private schools.[17] Among
the women, 12 had attended state schools and 11 had attended private,
with no significant variation by party. Only three women did not supply
this information in their official biographies.

TABLE 1-C

*Age in Year of Election
Comparison of Women and Men M.P.s
All Parties, 1970*

	Women		Men	
Age	Number	Percent	Number	Percent
Below 36	3	12	20	3
36-50	11	42	239	39.5
51-64	10	39	232	38.4
Over 64	2	8	83	13.7
Unknown	0	0	30	5
Total	*26*	*101*	*604*	*99.6*

SOURCE: See Appendix

In terms of higher education, the backgrounds of men and women
were similar. Seventy-six percent of the men and 73% of the women
attended some university or college.

The occupational groupings of the men and women were also similar. The largest groups of men (59%) and women (66%) were in the
professions. The second largest grouping of men (33%) was manual
workers. For the women the second largest group (19%) was "not
employed," i.e., held no salaried positions. Only 7% of the men and
15% of the women held political jobs.

As in 1929 and 1945, a higher percentage of women M.P.s had been
elected to political office before entering the House of Commons (62%
of the women and 31% of the men). And once again a larger percentage
of women had been active within their parties (92% of the women and
38% of the men).

In 1970 the number of successful women candidates entering the
House of Commons on their second attempt was the same as first-time
winners (31%). Only slightly fewer (27%) were successful on their
third attempt. For the men, on the other hand, 68% won on their first
try, 16% on their second, and 11% on their third.

In forming their government, the Conservatives were not as generous
with cabinet positions as the Labor Party had been in 1945. Only one

women was so honored: Margaret Thatcher, Secretary of State for Education and Science. Priscilla, Lady Tweedsmuir was named Minister of State for Scotland, but this is not a cabinet post. (Nine Labor women had been appointed to ministerial posts in the preceding Labor government.)

TABLE 2-C

Education of Women and Men M.P.s
All Parties, 1970

	Women		Men	
Education	Number	Percent	Number	Percent
University	19	73	462	76
Abroad	1	4	7	1
Non/unknown	6	23	135	22
Total	*26*	*100*	*604*	*99*

SOURCE: See Appendix

TABLE 3-C

Occupation in Year of Election
Comparison of Women and Men M.P.s
All Parties, 1970

	Women		Men	
Occupation	Number	Percent	Number	Percent
Political*	4	15	40	7
Professional†	17	66	361	59
Manual worker	0	0	203	33
Not employed	5	19	0	0
Unknown	0	0	0	0
Total	*26*	*100*	*604*	*99*

*Elected office holders, union organizers, and civil servants.
†Professions include law, teaching, journalism, medicine, and theater. Positions in business are at the management level.
SOURCE: See Appendix

TABLE 4-C

Experience in Local Government
Comparison of Women and Men M.P.s
All Parties, 1970

	Women		Men	
	Number	Percent	Number	Percent
Elected office	16	62	185	30.6
No elected office	10	39	407	67
Unknown	0	0	12	1.9
Total	*26*	*101*	*604*	*99.5*

SOURCE: See Appendix

TABLE 5-C

Comparison of Women and Men M.P.s
All Parties, 1970

	Women		Men	
	Number	Percent	Number	Percent
Party worker	24	92	229	37.9
Not a party worker	2	8	363	60
Unknown	0	0	12	1.9
Total	*26*	*100*	*604*	*99.8*

SOURCE: See Appendix

TABLE 6-C

Number of Campaigns Before First Election to Parliament
Comparisons of Women and Men M.P.s
All Parties, 1970

Number of Previous	Women		Men	
Campaigns	Number	Percent	Number	Percent
0	8	31	410	68
1	8	31	99	16
2	7	27	65	11
3	2	8	20	3
4	0	0	3	1[a]
5	1	4	0	0
6	0	0	1	0[b]
7	0	0	0	0
Unknown	0	0	6	1
Total	*26*	*101*	*604*	*100*

[a]Slightly less than 0.5
[b]Negligible

SOURCE: See Appendix

Conclusion

In comparisons of the men and women elected to the House of Commons in these three general elections, is it possible to discern any significant trends? It is important to remember that the 1929 and 1945 elections were held in unusual circumstances. In 1929 no one could predict how newly enfranchised women would vote. In 1945 the election reflected the upheavals of war. In both these elections the Labor Party was victorious. In 1970, a more "normal" year, the election was viewed less as a victory for the Conservatives than a defeat for Labor.

Over the years the total number of candidates from both major parties has steadily increased. The 1970 election had one exception: there was a decline in the number of Labor women candidates standing. For the weakened Liberal Party, there has been a steady decline of candidates, but the minor parties have shown a steady increase in both male and female candidates. Although there has been a slight increase in the number of women elected to Parliament over the years (fourteen in 1929; twenty-four in 1945; twenty-six in 1970), the percentages of successful women candidates have actually declined. In 1929, 30% of all women candidates won seats. This dropped to 25% in 1945 and rose slightly to 26% in 1970. (See chapter 4, p. 52) For men there has been a steady decline. Fifty-eight percent of all male candidates won in 1929; 38% in 1945, and 34% in 1970. This implies that male candidates in the earlier years were more secure politically once they had their parties' nomination.

Average ages for M.P.s have not followed a discernible pattern. In the three elections under study, the average age for men was highest in 1929 (50.5), when the average age for women was the lowest (46.5). Male M.P.s may have been older because so many young men had died in World War I. In 1945, the average for women was higher than for the men (51 and 46, respectively). World War II had not taken as high a death toll as in World War I, and younger men were actively courted by the parties. In the election of 1970, the mean average for men and women was in the late forties.

Educational information has become increasingly available with each of the elections as more detailed records are being kept by the parties. It was difficult to locate secondary school information, however. For men, the private school attended was more important than the university. The percentage of members who attended private schools has remained high, regardless of which party is in the majority. In the 1929 election 43% of the M.P.s had private school educations. Educational information for women M.P.s was scanty.

In 1945, with a tremendous Labor majority, 32% of the male members were educated in private schools, but none of the Labor women were. In 1970, the percentage of male M.P.s with private school backgrounds was still high (31%). A large percentage of women (42%) were educated in private schools.

In all elections, a higher percentage of women than men M.P.s have had a college or university education. Percentages for men with such training have been on the rise. In 1929 71% of the women and 43% of the men had university backgrounds. In 1970 the percentage for women was 77%, for men, 78%.

The occupations of M.P.s have changed over the years. In 1929, 48% of the men were in the professions, whereas the largest percentage of women M.P.s held political jobs. In 1945, roughly one-half of both groups were in the professions, with political jobs a close second. In 1970 the professions still accounted for the largest percentages, but for the men the second strongest category was "manual worker." For the women, the second largest group were not employed. This increase in professional standing in perhaps a reflection of the increase in higher education. Fewer M.P.'s hold political jobs. In other words, fewer professional trade unionists are being elected to Parliament.

If we compare the number of times a candidate ran for the House of Commons before winning a seat, we find the position of women declining. In 1929, 50% of the women won on their first effort. In 1970, only 31% were successful on their first try. Male candidates have fared better. In 1929, 59% of the men M.P.s had been successful on their first attempt. This may reflect the parties' attitude toward men and women candidates. A higher percentage of men are being nominated by their parties for safe seats. The Labor party is clearly the more sympathetic to women. They were the first to appoint a woman to a Cabinet post and have consistently appointed more women to office.[18] They have also nominated more women candidates for Parliament, although the Conservatives have a better overall record for nomiating women for safe seats. (See chapter 4.)

Before 1945, M.P.s were members of the "privileged classes," either through their social positions or their positions in trade unions.[19] Opportunities for new candidates are growing, however, as the number of trade-union-sponsored candidates declines and the Conservative party continues to seek new talent.

Successful candidates from the two major parties tend to fall into two occupational groupings. A majority of Conservative M.P.s are businessmen and lawyers. The majority of Labor M.P.s are teachers and journalists.[20]

Many observers believe that candidates for Parliament should have certain required credentials. Professor Harold Laski and Ellen Wilkinson proposed that service in local government be mandatory.[21]

Although women M.P.s have consistently been more experienced in local government than male M.P.s, and more active in party work, they have not received favored treatment from their parties. Male candidates have been given more safe seats to contest, and, consequently, win more frequently on their first political campaigns. Most political writers agree that "under the present system it is a party that decides the results in all but a few marignal cases."[22]

Part Three:

CONCLUSION

7

A Continuing Practice
of Discrimination

An analysis of women who ran for Parliament during the past fifty-two years reveals one pervasive factor, the continuing practice of discrimination on the part of the political parties. Women candidates have been allowed to run for relatively few safe seats. In discussing the parties' attitude toward the selection of candidates, *The Times*, observed with tongue in cheek that Labor women were given "the opportunity of converting the rural populations," and Conservative women "appear to specialize in the coalfields and East of London. Women are often told that they enjoy martyrdom; if that is so, they must feel grateful to their party headquarters for these opportunities for self-indulgence."[1] My research confirms the importance of running for a seat held by one's party—women candidates were elected in 79% of the cases in which they ran for a seat held by their party, compared with only 11% of the cases in which they ran for a seat not held by their party.

The Pioneer women, that is, those elected prior to 1945, were aware of the discrimination against women. The National Council for Equal Citizenship studied the fifty-three contests in the 1935 General Election involving Conservative, Labor, and Liberal women candidates. They found that in these fifty-three constituencies there had been 318 election contests from 1918 until 1935. In these 318 contests, there had been only twenty-seven wins (9%) by the women's own parties. The researchers then compared these results with seats contested in 1935 by twice as many unsuccesful male candidates, chosen at random. They found that these unsuccessful male candidates were contesting seats in 1935 that had been won by their own parties in 19% of the elections from 1918 to 1935. In other words, in the 1935 election, both the winning and losing women candidates from the three major parties had contested seats that were on the average less likely to be won by their parties than were the seats contested by the unsuccessful men.[2] Although these statistics were gathered during the Pioneer period, my research suggests that the Modern period, that is, 1945 and later, has brought no change in attitudes. Only twenty-six (7%) of the 373 women candidates standing for Parliament in the Modern Group were standing for seats held immediately prior to the election by their parties.

Because women are relatively new to politics, the attitude of each party is critical. Overall, the Labor Party has selected more women candidates than the Conservative Party and has had more women elected. However, in the Pioneer Group the Conservative Party consistently had a higher percentage of their women candidates elected. This higher percentage reflects the fact that eight of the seventeen Conservative M.P.s stood for a seat vacated by their husbands. In the Pioneer Group so many women entered Parliament by their husbands' seats when the husbands entered the House of Lords that the *Manchester Guardian* felt it necessary to issue a warning: "It may yet be expedient to check the growing vested interest of the Second Chamber in the representative House."[3] (At the time, four of the fifteen women members had husbands in the House of Lords.) But another view was that the women were well prepared for the job because they had been "active workers in their husbands' constituencies."[4]

The Conservative record is not as good in the Modern Period. Although the Conservative Party won four General Elections (1951, 1955, 1959, and 1970), only in the last two have the Conservatives elected a higher percentage of their women candidates than Labor.

The fact that the Liberal Party has generally fielded a higher percentage of women candidates reinforces the theory that the more hopeless candidacies are those most widely available to women. For example, in the 1945 election thirty women ran as Liberals, or nine percent of the total of 307 Liberal candidates. On the other hand, Labor, which invariably proposed more women candidates than the Conservatives, had only forty women candidates (6%) in a total of 604, while the Conservatives had only fourteen out of 573 candidates (2%).

The parties have defended this poor record on two counts: the shortage of potential women candidates and a negative reaction to women candidates by the electorate, especially women voters. This argument seems specious because the voters tend to vote for party rather than candidates.[5] Researchers assert that British voters tend to "acquire an identification with one or another political party at a fairly early age" and "tend to retain this identification throughout their lives"; hence, the party's selection of a seat for a candidate would seem to be crucial to the success of that candidate.[6] This, of course, is consistent with my finding that, of the forty-seven women from all political parties who ran from 1918 to 1970 for seats already held by their party, some thirty-seven (79%) won. Furthermore, the ten who lost were members of the party that went down to national defeat at that particular election.

As for the attitude of the women voters, the candidates whom I interviewed, both successful and unsuccessful, unanimously agreed that they had received the wholehearted support of the women from their own parties within their constituencies. Further, they received the most careful questioning from the women on the committees that chose candidates. The women candidates attributed these relentless examinations to the fact that their examiners were familiar with the personal problems that would confront a woman candidate and wanted to know if the prospective candidate was aware of the pitfalls of a political career.

The selection committee for a "safe" constituency must interview many applicants when the seat becomes vacant. There may be as many as four hundred applicants, as compared with twenty for a marginal seat and four or five for a hopeless seat. Yet, because an incumbent typically keeps a safe seat for quite a while, these constituency committees have had little experience in selecting a candidate; hence, they are often not qualified to evaluate fully all the candidates in order to locate the best qualified.[7]

Pressures, both within and without the constituencies, are brought to bear on the selection committees. Parties often award safe seats to party leaders in order to guarantee their return to Parliament, or they award them to loyal party members or to promising young politicians. In the Labor Party, union influence is an important factor. Susan Lawrence suggested that "there is a tendency on the part of trade unions to regard Parliamentary seats as comfortable retiring places for the veterans of the movement."[8] The unions contribute both voter strength and money to the party. This influence is detrimental to women candidates, because unions usually support a man who has worked within their ranks.[9] Yet, the influence was not insurmountable when Judith Hart was a candidate for the Lanark constituency. The left-wing section of the constituency supported her candidacy, but the local miners' union supported a male candidate. The miners' delegates to the selection committee who favored her candidacy intentionally failed to appear when the voting occurred. Their absence gave her a majority of the votes. Had they come to the meeting, they would have been compelled to vote for the male union candidate.

There is no question that potential women candidates are not numerous. There has never been the same ratio of women candidates to women voters as there has been for men. Although the number of women candidates has grown from seventeen in 1918 to sixty-seven in 1935, the number elected showed a much smaller corresponding rise in absolute numbers. One woman was elected in 1918, only nine in 1935. The election in 1945 marked the greatest increase of women M.P.s: twenty-four were elected. Still, the number of women M.P.s has remained relatively stable up to the present time, as have the number of women candidates who stand for Parliament. Only once—in 1950—has the total number of women candidates exceeded one hundred in a General Election. (There were 126.)

Can this poor showing by the parties be attributed solely to party discrimination? Ellen Wilkinson thought so.[10] Monica Whately accused the parties of reserving "all the safe seats for male members" so that in time women "lose their enthusiasm for fighting."[11] Yet many of the Modern women candidates deny discrimination on the part of their parties, even though the same women admit that a woman candidate must be better than a male competitor in order to secure selection in a constituency. This attitude is particularly prevalent among the Labor candidates. The Countess of Longford wrote that "there was no prejudice against a woman," but of her 1935 candidacy for Cheltenham, she said, "Everyone in the constituency felt that a woman was just right for a hopeless seat."[12]

A woman candidate must be dedicated, and determined to stand. One of the Conservative candidates described the campaign of Sally Oppenheim, Conservative M.P., who, as the wife of a millionaire, used her money in order to build a successful campaign in spite of the lukewarm support she received from her party. Although she is a very capable woman, the Conservative Party has not appointed her to any immediate post. It was the Party's fear that she would offend the voters, yet a Conservative male who is wealthy is treated differently.

There seems little doubt that if women were given more safe seats to contest, and thus had a better chance to make a showing, other women would be encouraged to stand for office. However, there are several other factors that hold women back. As Lady Summerskill said, "Social customs, from time immemorial, have been very stronger than law."[13] Society still expects women to bear the major responsibility for maintaining their homes and raising their children. This, of course, means that it is very difficult for women to spend the amount of time in London that Parliamentary duties require. Parliament is in session from 2:30 P.M. until 11:00 P.M.; a definite handicap that was mentioned by several of the women whom I interviewed. Judith Hart noted that if Labor is reelected, there is hope that they will be able to change the hours.

Before 1939, only a shortage of money prevented women from hiring domestic help, but "the war ended this and now none are available."[14] Joan, Lady Davidson, said that, had she had to cope with today's shortage of domestic help, she would have never been able to enter politics.[15] Edith, Lady Summerskill said that she would never have accepted a constituency outside of London. Furthermore, "Nana," who helped to raise her daughter, Shirley, joined her daughter's household so that she, too, could enter politics.[16] One ray of light in this area would be the increase of nursery and school accommodations. Additionally there is need for a true partnership between husband and wife in sharing household responsibilities.

The marriages of women candidates often suffer as a result of their political careers. Lady Summerskill insisted that women have no hope unless they choose a husband possessing two qualities—unselfishness and intelligence, provided intelligence is "not the companion of vanity."[17] After meeting Lady Summerskill's husband, I believe her experience was the basis for her formula. Dr. Samuels is both intelligent and very supportive of her career. The women I talked with were very open about the stress that political life has placed on their marriages. Judith Hart stated that her career was possible because her husband was able to relocate in London. Each woman knew of several marriages that had ended because of the wives' political commitments. The Countess of Longford described her withdrawal from a promising Labor constituency because her husband had been given a hopeless seat to fight. She said her "feminist armour suddenly fell apart. I just could not see him keeping the home fires burning while I set the Thames on fire at Westminster."[18] The Liberal candidate, Margaret Winfield, said that she would not want to be in Parliament now because her husband has retired and would not like to see her so occupied.[19]

The guilt that career women often feel makes them redouble their efforts to be "good wives and mothers." Thus, they overwork in every sphere. Margaret Laing quoted a survey taken of English women holding top administrative offices that showed that more than half of the married women felt that "their work had a deleterious effect on their health."[20] She concluded that until women were trained "to feel new satisfactions without old guilts," as well as learning "how to satisfy their increasingly varied interests, without defeating or draining themselves in the process," there will be no substantial increases in the number of women pursuing a serious career.[21]

Both male and female candidates face the problem of financing a political career. They must either be financially independent or have an occupation that allows them to attend Parliament and to spend time with their constituents. In the past, they have also had to have sufficient funds to pay their own campaign expenses. The parties have solved this problem for the candidates, however. Up until 1947 the Conservative candidate had to pay all expenses. In 1939 Mrs. Mavis Tate, Conservative M.P., who had separated from her husband in 1938, had to decline to stand for the Frome seat because "her financial position has very much altered."[22] Now that constituency associations are responsible for financing campaigns, candidates are now allowed to contribute more than £25 per year and M.P.s no more than £50. The Labor candidate has traditionally had an easier financial burden to bear. Many candidates were sponsored by either a trade union or a cooperative society, which would then pay election expenses. The unsponsored Labor candidate's campaign expenses are the concern of the local constituency party, but he or she gets some help from the central party funds.

The women candidates have the added expense of household help. Judith Hart, Labor M.P., said that nearly half of her salary is used for this purpose. In many cases, however, women have the advantage of not being the sole support of their families.

In order to examine statistically the charge that parties discriminate against women, I compared the statistics of the men and women elected to Parliament in three General Elections (1929, 1945, and 1970). In these three Elections, only one-quarter of the women candidates were elected as M.P.s, whereas one-third of the male candidates were elected. To be sure, in the Pioneer Group, the parties gave many safe seats to women, sometimes as successors to their husbands; fifty percent of the women (1929) were successful in their first election effort, the same percentage as for men. But, with the decline of safe seats assigned to women in the Modern Period, this percentage in 1970 fell to only 30% for women compared with 68% for men. Yet the elected women members in the three General Elections under study seem better qualified than the men members, according to several measures. A larger percentage of the women had held local elected political offices, showing a steady rise from 43% (1929) up to 62% (1970). For the same period, the record for men ranges from only 22% (1929) up to 30% (1970). The women were much more active party workers, in the ninetieth percentile or above in all elections, whereas the men ranged from only 16% (1929) to a high of 38% (1970). In the early election, the women were considerably better educated than their male counterparts (72% attended college, compared to 43% of the men). Over the years, however, the men have closed the gap; by 1970 the two groups were equal in educational attainments.

Women as Politicians

The role that women see for themselves in political affairs has undergone a definite change during the period under study. The Pioneer women M.P.s began their Parliamentary duties motivated by suffragist ideals—political, economic, and social. They refused to be intimidated by the designations "only a woman M.P.," and attacked legal and political discrimination against women wherever it occurred. In the same year that women received a limited franchise, Parliament passed a bill allowing women to stand for Parliament at age twenty-one. Women M.P.s fought to enlarge the municipal franchise to include married women. In order to improve women's economic situation they fought to have the Government Sex Disqualification Removal Bill passed. This opened the legal profession to women, and led to the appointment of women magistrates. Women could now serve on juries. Organizations such as the Society of Chartered Accountants had to admit women. Women had to fight harder to win Civil Service opportunities (1921). The decade of the twenties saw a yearly advance of legal equality for women. By 1928, when women were granted an equal franchise, a major hurdle had been passed. This new freedom brought recognition of wide differentiation within the sex—the old presumption that all women are alike was discredited.

Though they demanded equality, women M.P.s did not find it demeaning to "enter political life for the defense of interests which are considered to be their special concern."[23] In 1932, Mary Pickford, M.P. for Hammersmith North, explained that women did represent the whole community. Because all members "speak out on subjects of which they have real knowledge," she said, women often "speak with authority on social questions."[24] By the 1940s, women members had taken the lead in social legislation.[25] These issues included "housing, public health in all its aspects, education, the care of children, the provision of information and assistance to mothers, even aid in old age and invalidity for men and women."[26] Although much progress has been made, women still blame legal injustice on the fact that law and politics are male-dominated professions. Nevertheless, women agree that the early barriers raised against women were more susceptible to change than "the domestic, institutional and social customs that keep women in the home."[27]

Although most were originally interested primarily in domestic legislation, women M.P.s were alert to the Fascist threat that began in the 1930s. They did not hesitate to broaden their political activities, as illustrated by the activities of Ellen Wilkinson, the Duchess of Atholl, and Eleanor Rathbone. The wide range of women's expertise has continued to grow as more professions and educational opportunities have opened to them, and much of the more pressing social legislation has been successfully completed.

The two major parties have tended to view their women supporters differently. The Conservative Party had traditionally encouraged women to work in the women's sections, whereas the Labor Party has always allowed women to be actively engaged in party policy. Five seats on the National Executive Committee of the Labor Party are reserved for women. Judith Hart said that younger candidates today are coming up the ladder via direct party involvement and are not going into local government. Local statistics show that regardless of Party, in 1968 "only 12% of the councillors are women."[28] Again, Labor, under the leadership of Prime Minister Harold Wilson in the 1960s, was the first to recognize women's diverse abilities beyond domestic issues when he appointed Barbara Castle as Minister of Overseas Development and Eirene White as Minister of State for Foreign Affairs. The Conservatives still tend to appoint women for the Ministry of Education, e.g., Margaret Thatcher, under the administration of Edward Heath, although she is a specialist on social insurance. (There was speculation that she could have been appointed Chancellor of the Exchequer had the Conservatives won the October 1974 General Election.) Mrs. Thatcher has now become leader of the Conservative Party, with the possibility that she may become the first woman chief executive of a modern Western nation.

Generally, once a woman candidate is accepted by her party, and elected, the party is loyal to her. The parties support their women incumbents' reelection, just as they do their male incumbents, until they create a disturbance within the party. There have not been many women who suffered this fate. In the Pioneer Period, the Duchess of Atholl broke with the Conservative Party over the Spanish Civil War, and subsequently lost her seat when a new Conservative candidate was selected to oppose her. In the Modern Period, Margaret McKay, Labor M.P. for Clapham, was rejected by the General Council of the Clapham constituency Labor Party after they had secured the national executive's permission to ask her to step down. The decision was taken because she "does not devote enough time to constituency matters," but she said, "had I supported the Israeli cause the Clapham situation would never have arisen."[29] The Clapham Labor party refused to answer her charge, but their action was taken shortly after Mrs. McKay had signed a pro-Arab newspaper advertisement.

In a comparison between the successful women of Group I and Group II, we find definite changes. During the Pioneer years, the Conservative women candidates were largely selected because of family influence. This has dropped from 71% to 38% in the Modern years. It is reflected in a corresponding drop in women candidates' success on their first parliamentary effort, down from 81% of the Pioneers to 48% of the Moderns. The Conservative Modern women are also younger, with an average age of forty-three, and are more career-oriented (86%).

A very large percentage (62%) of the Conservative Moderns are either unmarried (38%) or widows (24%). Of the women, only 45% have children. When Patricia Hornsby Smith was asked if being married was a disadvantage, she replied, "No, in fact I would say the reverse is true. It must take a very understanding tolerant man to be an M.P.'s husband."[30] On the other hand, two Modern Conservative members, Beatrice Wright and Patricia Ford, have resigned their seats because of the need to give more time to their children.

The Labor Party has not had such a drastic reversal of family influence, dropping from 60% of the Pioneer Group to 50% of the Moderns who were members of politically active families. There is a corresponding drop from 50% (Pioneers) to 36% (Moderns) of the Labor women who won on their first try. The characteristics of the Labor women candidates are changing. A very high proportion (69%) of the Moderns are married, and another 16% are widows, compared with the Pioneers with only 44% married and 6% widows. Of this 85%, 60% have children, whereas only 33% of the Pioneers did. This may be a result of the higher age of Labor women M.P.s, an average of forty-seven, up from forty-four. Doris Fisher, for example, explained that "when the children were well established in school I then felt that I had relinquished a few responsibilities and could go into government."[31] Jennie Adamson promised that "our new home will not suffer because I have a new sphere of usefulness."[32] Whatever their family responsibilities or their personal feelings, women candidates seem to have found it necessary to explain to their constituents that their home lives would not be compromised by their political activities.

After comparing the careers of the women who won with the candidates who lost, what route could be advocated for potential candidates? Extensive party work and experience in elected office are two key factors, both seemingly more important for women than for men. However, if the unsuccessful woman candidate has a great deal of perseverance and continues to stand despite repeated failures, she has a good chance of eventually winning. Up to the present time, so many unsuccessful women candidates have become discouraged that they have removed their names from the available candidates list; thus 22% of the women standing for a third time win their elections, as compared with 10% on their second effort. If more women were willing to stand for a third time, this percentage of successful candidates would no doubt decline.

For the prospective Conservative woman candidate in the Pioneer Group, family influence was very important; 47% of the successful women did come from politically active families, compared with 4% of the unsuccessful candidates. In the Modern Group, none of the successful women had family influence, and only 5% of the unsuccessful women did. This area dropped in importance as experience in elective office became more important.

The successful Conservative women recognized the need for party work, and in both the Pioneer and Modern Groups 88% of them were active. The unsuccessful women in the Pioneer Group were not very active (17%) in the party, but in the Modern Group their participation has increased to 67%.

The rise in importance of elective office is evident. In the Pioneer Group both successful and unsuccessful Conservative women included only 17% who had held an elected political office prior to standing for Parliament. Although the percentage increased for both successful and unsuccessful women in the Modern Group, the successful women made the greatest gains, with 64% having held elective office compared with 44% of the unsuccessful women.

The Labor women candidates' success in Pioneer Group reflected the importance of family influence: 38% of the successful women candidates came from politically active families as compared with only 2% of the unsuccessful women. However, the amount of influence dropped in the Modern Group to only 12% of the successful candidates, and 4% for the unsuccessful. The unsuccessful Labor woman candidate did not increase her experience either in party work or in elected political office. Whereas 90% of the Labor women (both Pioneer and Modern) who were successful worked in their party, only 27% of the Pioneer and Modern unsuccessful candidates contributed their efforts. Furthermore, while 60% of the successful Labor women (both Pioneer and Modern) had previously been elected to political office, only 33% of the unsuccessful candidates in each group had the same experience.

Three Remarkable Women

The careers of the Duchess of Atholl, Ellen Wilkinson, and Eleanor Rathbone reflect the different political paths taken by the Pioneer women who came from different backgrounds and parties.

The Duchess of Atholl, an aristocratic Conservative, originally opposed the suffragist efforts to gain the vote. She herself had no political ambitions, working within the Women's Section of the Conservative Party only in order to increase party support for her husband. Her husband entered the House of Commons and in 1917 moved into the House of Lords. In 1923 the leader of the local Conservative Party Association asked the Duchess to stand for West Perthshire and Kinross. She won the election and remained an M.P. until 1938, even holding her seat in 1929 when Labor won.

During the years preceding her Parliamentary career, she was involved in philanthropic and charitable work. Once she entered Parliament she was a disciplined Conservative member. She accepted her party's rejection of independence for India, for example, and their refusal to raise the school-leaving age for children from fourteen to fifteen because industry needed child laborers. Her loyal party support was recognized when she was appointed Parliamentary Secretary to the Board of Education. Even though the position carried no real responsibility, she was the first Conservative woman to hold Ministerial rank. She was the only woman M.P. to vote against the petition that the "Distinguished Strangers" Gallery be opened to women, again following her party. But she recognized that women were "paying the penalty of insisting on equality of status with men"—they were not being given much opportunity to speak in the House.[33]

With the rise of Communism and Fascism in the 1930s, the Duchess broadened her horizons. She made her first foreign policy speech in 1936, and by 1937 she was concerned primarily with foreign affairs. Her support of the Spanish Republican cause led her into close working relationships with both Ellen Wilkinson and Eleanor Rathbone. The three women made several trips together to Europe and worked together on committees.

The Duchess's refusal to support the Conservative Party's foreign policy position with regard to the war in Spain led the Unionist Association in her district to seek a new candidate. She immediately resigned from Parliament and campaigned as an Independent. She was defeated in the 1938 election by the Conservative candidate and never reentered political life.

Ellen Wilkinson came from a working-class background. Very early in her career she became a loyal member of the Labor Party after a brief flirtation with the Communist Party. An outspoken opponent of all forms of discrimination, she never became a militant suffragist but supported the Labor Party position of an equal franchise for all adults, not one based on property requirements.

Miss Wilkinson pursued a university education on scholarships, before embarking on a career as a trade union organizer. Even after election to the City Council of Manchester she maintained her diligent party work. Her ability was recognized by the Labor Party and she was given numerous positions of importance. Her first parliamentary effort in 1923 failed, but within a year the Labor Party offered her the industrial constituency of Middlesborough. Here she was successful and served from 1924 until Labor was swept from the government in the General Election of 1931. She was selected by the constituency of Jarrow in the next General Election of 1935 and served in Parliament until her death in 1947. In 1945, Clement Attlee had named her Minister of Education. This made her the second woman to hold a Cabinet post.

Throughout her parliamentary career, Miss Wilkinson opposed capitalism because of its economic discrimination against the working class. She also opposed British imperialism as a form of discrimination. She joined the feminists in their efforts to gain full equality for women, and was described as a "specialist in aggressions, and a hard hitting fighter...."[34]

Eleanor Rathbone's background was similar in some ways to that of both the Duchess of Atholl and Ellen Wilkinson. Like the Duchess she was socially and financially secure. Like Miss Wilkinson her political views and activities were distinctly left-wing.

Miss Rathbone was a typical suffragist from a middle-class background. Before her election to Parliament in 1929 as the Independent M.P. from the Combined English Universities she had served as president of the National Society for Equal Citizenship for ten years. She was one of the early feminists to contend that women must not only overcome discrimination but must develop new paths for themselves rather than following the trails already familiar to men.

Miss Rathbone's family background in philanthropic activity led her into active social work. She later served as a Justice of the Peace and became the first woman member elected to the Liverpool City Council. Her family's wealth had enabled her to make her own choice of a career after attending Oxford; she was one of the first women to do so.

She was especially concerned with destroying economic discrimination against women and spent her entire parliamentary career securing the passage of a Family Allowance Plan, with the funds to be paid directly to the mothers. Her compassion led her into efforts to help the European refugees from political upheavals of the 1930s. Her efforts to end discrimination against women extended to the Middle East, Africa, and India, as she attempted to make the government more responsive to the suffering of women throughout the empire.

Summary

The evidence of more than fifty years shows that the voting patterns of the British people have changed very little despite the presence of women in the House of Commons. Voters have followed traditional divisions based on class, rather than sex. In fact, women candidates for Parliament have not been spared opposition from members of their own sex. Lady Tarrington, a Conservative "Pioneer," complained that "she suffered great annoyance during the election from organized interruptions by women belonging to a party opposed to her."[35] Nor did women politicians encourage unity under the banner of sex. Alice, Lady Bacon, formerly M.P. and Minister of State at the Home Office, probably spoke for all her female colleagues when she said, "There is no such thing as a woman M.P."[36]

The ninety-four women who have served in Parliament during the past fifty-two years can be credited with destroying much of the legal and political discrimination against women. They have also tried to end social and economic discrimination although these are much harder to root out. Despite their success in securing such legislation as Eleanor Rathbone's Family Allowance Plan, however, they have not been able to exercise any real sustained influence on Parliament because of their small numbers.[37]

A report prepared by the Labor Party attributed the small number of women M.P.s to the "biological function of women as child-bearers," maintaining that their consequent position at the center of the family brings its own peculiar limitations. And, of course, the attitudes of many people—both men and women—have not kept pace with the removal of legal restrictions.[38] As more women are choosing careers outside the home, they are shaking off the patterns of the past. This independence in choosing new lifestyles may conceivably enlarge the number of women involved in politics. The parties will be challenged to respond by offering women more plausible constituencies. However, there is little indication that the number of women candidates or the number of women M.P.s will increase substantially in the immediate future.

Appendix:
Methodology

Following is a description of the data recorded on computer punch cards for all successful women candidates, all unsuccessful women candidates, and the male candidates in the general elections of 1929, 1945, and 1970.

Successful Women Candidates

1. *Party* Women stood for the following parties: Conservative, Independent, Labor, Liberal, National Conservative, Scottish Nationalist, and Unionist. The National Conservative, Unionist, and Conservative parties were grouped together as Conservative.
2. *Birth* The year of birth of each woman member was listed.
3. *Death* For deceased women in this category, the year of death was listed; these statistics were not used in the study.
4. *Marriage* For married M.P.s, the year of marriage was listed if available. The year of a second marriage was also listed if available. If no date was available, it was shown only that the candidate was married.
5. *Children* The number of children was recorded.
6. *Honorary Degrees* Honorary degrees were listed; these statistics were not used in the study.
7. *Education* Primary education was listed. Secondary modern and secondary grammar schools were listed separately but in the study were recorded together as public schools. Secondary direct grant, secondary independent, and approved schools were listed separately, but were combined in the study, as private schools. For higher education, Oxford, Cambridge, and the London School of Economics were listed separately from other universities on the cards, but all were combined in the study as university education. Training colleges and teaching colleges were also listed separately but were combined in the study under college totals.
8. *Occupation* Seventeen different occupations were listed, as well as a "not employed" category. When more than one occupation was

129

listed for the same member, I chose the one she had prepared for educationally or had followed the longer period of time. The seventeen occupations were grouped in the study as professional/business and political.

9. *Ran and not elected*   Every election in which a candidate ran unsuccessfully was listed.
10. *Elected*   The year the candidate was elected.
11. *Second election*   If the candidate lost her seat and was reelected a second time.
12. *Husband M.P.*   If the candidate's husband was an M.P. when she was elected, or had ever been an M.P.
13. *Took his seat*   If the candidate took her husband's seat, either when he retired or died.
14. *Party held seat*   If the candidate's party held the seat in the previous election.
15. *Overturned opposition*   If the candidate won a seat that had been held in the preceding election by a member of another party.
16. *Father M.P.*   If the candidate's father had ever been an M.P.
17. *Took father's seat*   If the candidate took her father's seat when he retired or died.
18. *Mother M.P.*   If candidate's mother had ever been an M.P.
19. *Brother M.P.*   If candidate's brother had ever been an M.P.
20. *Active political family*   If a member of the candidate's close family (father, mother, sister, or brother) had ever been active in either politics or in trade unionism.
21. *Served in Parliament with husband*   Candidate and husband served in Parliament at the same time.
22. *Elected office*   The various local political offices (county and borough council, alderman, mayor) were all listed separately on the computer cards, but recorded in one category in the study.
23. *End of career*   How a candidate left office; whether she lost an election, resigned, or died. This material was not used in the study.
24. *Husband's occupation*   The occupation of the candidate's husband at the time of her election.
25. *Party office*   If the candidate held an office in her party or in the women's section of her party.
26. *Various organizations*   The Fabian and Co-op groups were listed, as well as university clubs.

Unsuccessful Women Candidates

The data recorded for each unsuccessful candidate were the same as described for the successful women candidates unless otherwise noted:

1. *Party* There were additional parties: Irish Nationalist, Welsh Nationalist, and Patriotic Party.
2. *Birth*
3. *Death*
4. *Marriage*
5. *Children*
6 *Honorary degrees* Not tabulated.
7. *Education*
8. *Occupation* There were more occupations noted on the cards, a total of thirty-two. The groupings in the study were the same as for successful candidates, however.
9. *Ran and not elected*
10. *Elected* Not applicable.
11. *Second election* Not applicable.
12. *Husband M.P.*
13. *Took his seat* Not applicable.
14. *Party held seat*
15. *Overturned opposition* Not applicable
16. *Father M.P.*
17. *Took father's seat* Not applicable.
18. *Mother M.P.* None
19. *Brother M.P.* None
20. *Active political party*
21. *Served in Parliament with husband* Not applicable
22. *Elected office*
23. *End of career* Not applicable.
24. *Husband's occupation* Too few observations available; not recorded.
25. *Party office*
26. *Various organizations*

*Observations in Addition to Those Tabulated
for Successful Women*

27. *Number of women in campaign*
28. *Widow*
29. *Seat changed parties but not to candidate*

Male Candidates Elected to Parliament

Less data were recorded for male candidates than for successful and unsuccessful women candidates, because only the information found in *Dod's Parliamentary Companion* was used, as follows:

2. *Birth*
7. *Education*   Only higher education was recorded
8. *Occupation*   Seventeen categories were listed. These were combined into four classifications: political, professional, manual worker, and not employed or unknown.
9. *Ran and not elected*
11. *Second election*
22. *Elected office*
23. *Party office*

Source of Data

Not surprisingly, more information was available for the ninety-four women who became members of Parliament than for those who were unsuccessful candidates. The very fact that little information is available on the latter group is significant, because it implies that their candidacies made little impact on the public.

When I began my research, only one volume of F. W. S. Craig's *British Parliamentary Elections* had been published.[1] The volume listed the candidates for Parliament from 1918-1949 and was an invaluable help. Neither the Conservative nor the Liberal Party libraries contained a complete listing of their women candidates. The Labor Party library, on the other hand, did have a complete record of all their candidates; the Labor Party library was also extremely useful because members of the staff have consistently clipped information published about prominent people in newspapers, regardless of party, from as early as the 1920s. For information on women involved in the elections held after 1949, I used *The Times Guide to the House of Commons.*[2] This meant a painstaking search through the Indexes of each General Election. Since women were listed as either "Miss" or "Mrs.," I was able to compile a complete listing, which I cross-checked after Craig's second volume was published in 1971.

To gather information on the men who were members of Parliament during the three election years chosen, I used *Dod's Parliamentary Companion,* which gives their party, age, education, professions, political experience, and the number of times they have run for Parliament.[3]

Interviews were held with women M.P.s both past and present, and with unsuccessful candidates. An attempt was made to interview a well-balanced group of women in terms of party and position. Edith, Lady Summerskill, former Labor M.P., and Joan, Lady Davidson, former Conservative M.P., are both now in the House of Lords. Lucy Middleton, a former Labor M.P., was chosen because she came from a working-class background. Two women are in the House of Commons (Lena Jeger and Judith Hart).

As the statistical material began to show the importance of party attitude toward women candidates, the need for interviews with unsuccessful candidates became evident. Three such candidates who agreed to be interviewed were: Millie Miller, Labor; Trixie Gardner, Conservative; and Margaret Winfield, Liberal.

Analytical Techniques

Because I had access to more than 20,000 separate pieces of data about more than 2,200 persons, I used a computer to aid in the analysis. My computer advisor, George Middleton, a Harvard graduate student, selected Fortran as the most appropriate language for this project.

Data on each person were coded on data sheets and then punched on cards. Mr. Middleton and I designed programs that instructed the computer regarding the calculations to make and the form in which to print the results. The diverse occupations of women candidates are a good illustration of the decision rules that I used to code categories of data—in this case, the "occupation" of the person under study. If a candidate had more than one occupation, I recorded the one pursued for the longest period of time. Because results are more meaningful when large samples are available, I combined areas of occupation in order to get three broad categories. These three were: "Political," which included office holders, union organizers, and civil servants; "Professions/Business," which included law, teaching, journalism, medicine, and the theater; and "Not Employed," which included married women who held no salaried position. The occupations of the husbands of women M.P.s fell into slightly different groupings: namely, "Politics," "The Professions," "Industry," and "Unskilled Workers."

The educational backgrounds of candidates illustrate another set of decisions made in coding. On the coding sheets, I listed all the schools attended by women candidates and M.P.s. I then used the computer to categorize the state schools as those that were either secondary modern or secondary grammar, and the private schools as those that were secondary direct grant, secondary independent, or approved schools.

Notes

Introduction

1. Ray Strachey, ed., *Five Women, Our Freedom and Its Results* (London: Hogarth Press, 1936), Chapter 1: "Changes in Public Life," by Eleanor Rathbone, p. 18.
2. Philippe Aries, *Centuries of Childhood: A Social History of Family Life,* trans. Robert Baldick (New York: Knopf, 1962).
3. This discussion of the suffragist movement is based chiefly on Kenneth Hudson, *Men and Women* (Newton Abbot, England: David & Charles, 1968); Josephine Kamm, *Rapiers and Battleaxes* (London: George Allen & Unwin, Ltd., 1966); William L. O'Neill, *The Woman Movement,* in *Historical Problems: Studies and Documents,* gen. ed. G. R. Elton (London: George Allen & Unwin, Ltd., 1969); E. Sylvia Pankhurst, *The Suffragette* (London: Gay and Hancock, Ltd., 1911); Constance Rover, *Women's Suffrage and Party Politics in Britain* (Toronto: University of Toronto Press, 1967); Ray Strachey, *Struggle: The Stirring Story of Women's Advance in England* (New York City: Duffield, 1930).
4. Rathbone, "Changes in Public Life," p. 22.
5. The Knights of the Shire were the smaller feudal landholders from the counties who were first summoned to a national council in 1262 under the Provisions of Oxford.
6. William O'Neill, *The Woman Movement,* in *Historical Problems, Studies and Documents,* ed. G. R. Elton (London: George Allen & Unwin, Ltd., 1969), p. 67.
7. Ray Strachey, *Struggle: The Stirring Story of Women's Advance in England* (New York City: Duffield, 1930), p. 344.

Chapter 1

1. The details of the Duchess of Atholl's life are taken from her autobiography, *Working Partnership* (London: Arthur Barker, 1958).
2. *Ibid.,* p. 32.
3. *Ibid.,* p. 171.
4. *Time Magazine,* 6 April 1936, p. 23.
5. Duchess of Atholl, *The Conscription of a People* (New York, Columbia University Press, 1931), p. 184.
6. Atholl, *Working Partnership,* pp. 135-136.
7. The first woman to hold a ministerial post was Margaret Bondfield, a Labor M.P.

8. Atholl, *Working Partnership*, p. 144.
9. *Ibid.*, p. 178.
10. *Time Magazine*, 6 April 1936, p. 29.
11. Atholl, *Conscription of a People*, p. 193.
12. Atholl, *Working Partnership*, p. 203.
13. *Ibid.*, p. 207.
14. *Ibid.*, p. 190.
15. *Ibid.*, p. 194.
16. *Ibid.*
17. Atholl, *Searchlight on Spain* (London: Purnell & Sons, 1938), p. 144.
18. *Ibid.*, p. 257; pp. 261-263; and Seton-Watson, *Britain and the Dictators* (New York: Macmillan Co., 1938), p. 369.
19. *Times* (London), 24 December 1936.
20. *Times* (London), 24 May 1937.
21. *Times* (London), 13 July 1937. Great Britain, Parliament, *Hansard's Parliamentary Debates* (Commons) 5th Series, 328 (1937): 1758-1761.
22. *Ibid.*, 326 (1937): 855; *Times* (London), 12 November 1937.
23. *Times* (London), 14 April 1937.
24. George Orwell, *Homage to Catalonia* (New York: Harcourt, Brace, 1952), p. 199.
25. Atholl, *Searchlight on Spain*, p. 212, *Times* (London), 17 April 1937, p. 14e.
26. *Times* (London), 24 April 1937.
27. Atholl, *Searchlight on Spain*, p. 137.
28. *Times* (London), 13 November 1937.
29. *Times* (London), 29 April 1938.
30. *Times* (London), 21 November 1938.
31. *Times* (London), 26 November 1938.
32. *Times* (London), 28 November 1938.
33. *Ibid.*
34. Mary D. Stocks, *Eleanor Rathbone* (London: Victor Gollancz, 1949), p. 255.
35. Atholl, *Working Partnership*, p. 229.
36. *Times* (London), 23 December 1938.
37. *Times* (London) 23 December 1938. *Annual Register* for 1938, p. 107.
38. Atholl, *Working Partnership*, p. 137.

Chapter 2

1. *Newcastle Journal*, 27 June 1938.
2. Interview with Edith, Lady Summerskill, London, 12 October 1971.
3. T. H. Shane, "The Rt. Hon. Ellen Wilkinson," *Pioneers and Founders* (clipping in Fawcett Library, n.d.).
4. *New York World*, 30 November 1924.
5. Cyril Clemens, *The Man from Limehouse: Clement Richard Attlee* (Missouri: International Mark Twain Society, 1946), p. 102.
6. Great Britain, Parliament, *Hansard's Parliamentary Debates* (Commons), 5th series, 414(1945):435.
7. *Oldhand Standard*, 11 December 1924.
8. *Graphic*, 13 November 1924.
9. *North East Daily Gazette*, 16 February 1925; *Northern Whig*, 31 July 1941; *San Francisco Examiner*, 26 January 1930; *Daily Telegraph*, 17 July 1941.

10. *Portsmouth Evening News,* 17 May 1928.
11. *Birkenhead News,* 10 January 1925.
12. *Northern Evening Dispatch,* 10 September 1928.
13. *Manchester Guardian,* 5 February 1930; *Western Mail,* 12 November 1924.
14. *Evening Standard,* 10 December 1924; *Yorks Evening News,* 10 December 1924.
15. *Northern Echo,* 21 February 1928.
16. *North East Daily Gazette,* 21 February 1928.
17. *Newcastle Chronicle,* 31 January 1927.
18. *Ibid.,* 28 March 1927.
19. *Evening Standard,* 14 May 1928.
20. *Liverpool Evening Express,* 25 November 1927.
21. *Glasgow Evening Citizen,* 22 February 1930.
22. *Hansard's* (Commons), 414 (1945):558.
23. *Northern Echo,* 7 December 1928.
24. *Hansard's* (Commons), 219(1928):974-75.
25. *North East Daily Gazette,* 6 July 1928.
26. *Hansard's* (Commons), 347(1939):283.
27. *Ibid.,* 360(1940):1018.
28. *Liverpool Daily Post,* 1 November 1938.
29. *Hull Evening News,* 29 January 1929.
30. *Bristol Evening Times,* 20 November 1928.
31. *Daily Express,* 14 December 1928.
32. *Ibid.,* 17 December 1928.
33. *Clarion,* 12 December 1924.
34. *Newcastle Sun,* 14 February 1925.
35. *Daily Herald,* 8 January 1925.
36. *Cambridge Press,* 15 November 1925.
37. *Hansard's* (Commons) 211 (1927):1385.
38. *Daily Express,* 1 March 1928.
39. *Evening Standard,* 20 March 1928.
40. *Ibid.,* 23 March 1928.
41. *Glasgow Bulletin,* 19 June 1929.
42. *Manchester Evening Chronicle,* 21 December 1928.
43. *Dispatch,* 6 April 1927.
44. *New York World,* 22 August 1926.
45. *Lancet,* 1 December 1928.
46. *Reynolds,* 17 May 1925.
47. *Ibid.*
48. *North East Daily Gazette,* 16 March 1925.
49. *Evening Standard,* 5 October 1926.
50. *North East Daily Gazette,* 17 January 1930.
51. *Ibid.,* 20 January 1930.
52. *Scotsman,* 28 October 1929.
53. *Halifax Daily Courier,* 20 June 1930.
54. *Daily Express,* 6 July 1933.
55. *Northern Echo,* 18 December 1933; *Manchester Guardian,* 7 November 1931.
56. *Surrey Mirror,* 10 June 1932.
57. *Ibid.*
58. *Patriot,* 9 May 1929.
59. *Southern Daily Echo,* 2 April 1931.

60. *Cheshire Daily Echo,* 10 March 1938.
61. *Daily Express,* 29 November 1932.
62. *Northern Daily Gazette,* 10 October 1934.
63. *Bolton Journal,* 5 October 1934.
64. *Ibid.*
65. *Daily Worker,* 15 November 1934.
66. *Evening Standard,* 15 November 1934.
67. *Walsall Observer,* 25 September 1937.
68. Clement R. Attlee, *As It Happened* (London: William Heinemann, 1954), p. 54.
69. *Dudley Herald,* 25 September 1937.
70. *News Chronicle,* 19 September 1938.
71. *East Kent Gazette,* 18 February 1939.
72. Kingsley Martin, "Ellen Wilkinson," *New Statesman and Nation,* 37 (15 February 1947):130.
73. *Newcastle Chronicle,* 31 March 1934.
74. *Cambridge Daily News,* 11 May 1932.
75. *Liverpool Daily News,* 11 May 1932.
76. *Shields News,* 9 October 1936.
77. *Cumberland Evening News,* 6 October 1936.
78. *Yorks Post,* 6 October 1936.
79. *Northern Echo,* 13 October 1936.
80. *Daily Dispatch,* 15 October 1936.
81. *Northeastern Chronicle,* 15 October 1936.
82. *Manchester Guardian,* 13 November 1936.
83. *East Kent Gazette,* 18 February 1939.
84. *Nottingham Gazette,* 22 January 1940.
85. *Hansard's* (Commons), 364(1940):1128.
86. *Yorks Post,* 23 September 1940.
87. *Cumberland Evening News,* 14 December 1939.
88. *Northern Echo,* 12 June 1942.
89. *News Chronicle,* 11 October 1940
90. *Manchester News Chronicle,* 25 April 1941.
91. *Ibid.,* 14 May 1941.
92. *Durham Chronicle,* 3 July 1942.
93. *Ibid.*
94. *Torquay Times,* 5 June 1942.
95. *Times,* 7 October 1942.
96. *News Chronicle,* 18 April 1944.
97. *New York Times Magazine,* 2 September 1945, pp. 20-21.
98. "Hire purchase" companies in England lend money.
99. Clemens, *The Man from Limehouse,* p. 87.
100. *Daily Herald,* 26 May 1945.
101. Francis Williams, *A Prime Minister Remembers: The War and Post-War Memoirs of the Rt. Hon. Earl Attlee* (London: William Heinemann, 1961), p. 8.
102. *Ibid.*
103. Hugh Dalton, *The Fateful Years: Memoirs 1931-1945* (London: Frederick Mullen, 1957), p. 224.
104. Herbert Morrison made no reference to Miss Wilkinson in his autobiography even though she had been a loyal supporter of his within the party and had ably served in his Ministry during the war years.
105. Attlee, *As It Happened,* p. 153; Williams, *A Prime Minister Remembers,* p. 80.

106. *Hansard's* (Commons), 414(1945):437.
107. *Times*, 19 June 1948.
108. *Times*, 6 February 1947.
109. *News Chronicle*, 8 February 1947.
110. *Daily Express*, 15 April 1929.
111. *Birmingham Sunday Mercury*, 13 October 1929.
112. Ellen Wilkinson, *The Town That Was Murdered* (London: Victor Gollancz, 1939), p. 191.
113. *Ibid.*, p. 18.
114. *Ibid.*, p. 19.
115. *Ibid.*, p. 26.
116. *Ibid.*, p. 28.
117. *Ibid.*, p. 81.
118. *Ibid.*, p. 123.
119. *Ibid.*, p. 134.
120. *Ibid.*, p. 189.
121. *Times*, 10 October 1930.
122. Ellen Wilkinson, *Peeps at Politicians* (London: Philip Allan & Co., Ltd., 1930), p. 7.
123. *Cheshire Daily Echo*, 10 March 1938.

Chapter 3

1. This seat, an anachronism that allowed plural voting, was finally abolished by Parliament in 1948. Prior to 1948, each university graduate had two votes in a general election: one for a candidate from the district where he or she resided, a second for a candidate from his or her university. The university ballots were mailed directly to the graduates by the registration offices of the universities.
2. Mary D. Stocks, *Eleanor Rathbone: A Biography* (London: Victor Gollancz, 1949), pp. 13-14.
3. *Spectator*, 11 January 1946.
4. William Rathbone's first wife, who died in 1859, bore five children. His second wife, Eleanor's mother, also had five children.
5. Stocks, *Eleanor Rathbone*, p. 53.
6. Lord Denning, *The Equality of Women*, Eleanor Rathbone Memorial Lectures (Liverpool: University of Liverpool Press, 1960), p. 1.
7. Stocks, *Eleanor Rathbone*, p. 51.
8. *Ibid.*, pp. 67-68.
9. *Evening Express*, 10 November 1922.
10. *Daily Post*, 11 November 1922.
11. *Evening Standard*, 6 November 1922.
12. *Evening Express*, 10 November 1922.
13. *Daily Post*, 5 November 1922.
14. *Ibid.*, 7 November 1922.
15. *Ibid.*, 4 November 1922.
16. *Evening Express*, 14 November 1922.
17. Eleanor F. Rathbone, *The Disinherited Family* (London: Edward Arnold & Co., 1924), p. 101.
18. *Ibid.*, p. 9.
19. *Ibid.*, p. 176.

20. *Ibid.*, p. 231.
21. *Ibid.*
22. Stocks, *Eleanor Rathbone*, pp. 95-96.
23. Eleanor Rathbone, "Changes in Public Life," in *Five Women*, ed. Ray Strachey (London: Hogarth Press, 1936), p. 56.
24. *Ibid.*, p. 58.
25. Rathbone, *Disinherited Family*, p. xl.
26. *Ibid.*, p. 63.
27. Eleanor Rathbone Papers, Letter to Constituents, 1939, XIV. 3.4, Harold Cohen Library, University of Liverpool, England.
28. *Ibid.*, Circular to Women Voters, XIV.3.3(10).
29. *Ibid.*, Letter to Constituents, 1929, XIV.3.4.
30. *Ibid.*, Letter to Constituents, 1935, XIV.3.4.
31. *Ibid.*, Statement to Minister of Labour, XIV.3.6(16).
32. *Ibid.*, Letters to Constituents, 1933, XIV.3.4.
33. Stocks, *Eleanor Rathbone*, p. 156.
34. Rathbone Papers, Circular Letter from India, 21 January 1932, XIV.1.7.
35. *Ibid.*, 9 February 1932, XIV.1.10.
36. *Ibid.*, Letter to Constituents, 1933, XIV.3.4.
37. Eleanor F. Rathbone, *Child Marriage: The Indian Minotaur* (London: George Allen & Unwin, Ltd., 1935), pp. 107 and 111.
38. Rathbone Papers, Letter to Constituents, 1934, XIV.3.4.
39. *Ibid.*, Letter to Constituents, 1935, XIV.3.4.
40. *Ibid.*
41. *Ibid.*, Vote of Censure Debate, 13 November 1933, XIV.3.6(14).
42. *Ibid.*, Letter to Constituents, 1934, XIV.3.4.
43. Pamela Brookes, *Women at Westminster* (London: Peter Davies, 1967), p. 112.
44. Rathbone Papers, Rights of Women in Palestine, XIV.2.5(57).
45. *Ibid.*, XIV.2.5(13).
46. *Ibid.*, XIV.2.5(14).
47. *Ibid.*, Letter to Constituents, 1935, XIV.3.4.
48. *Ibid.*, Letter to Constituents, 1938, XIV.3.4.
49. *Ibid.*
50. *Ibid.*, Opposition to the Nazis, XIV.2.6(16).
51. *Ibid.*, Campaign for Award of Nobel Peace Prize to Carl von Ossietzky, XIV.2.8(1-21).
52. *Ibid.*, Speech to Lambeth L.N.U., 5 June 1940, XIV.3.6(65).
53. *Ibid.*, Letter to Constituents, 1939, XIV.3.4.
54. *Ibid.*, Letter to Constituents, 1940, XIV.3.4.
55. *Ibid.*, Letter to Leonard E. Behrens, Esq., 29 January 1945, XIV.3.3. (37).
56. *Ibid.*, Letter to Lady Violet Bonham Carter, 6 February 1945, XIV.3.3. (34).
57. *Ibid.*, Letter to Eleanor Rathbone, 9 February 1945, XIV.3.3(34).
58. *Ibid.*, Letter to Constituents, 1939.

Chapter 4

1. *Times* (London), 29 November 1935.
2. *Manchester Guardian*, 10 October 1951.

3. Interview with Joan, Lady Davidson, London, 5 October 1971.
4. Ethel Wood, "Women in Parliament," *Sunday Telegraph*, 9 November 1944.
5. Interview with Joan, Lady Davidson, London, 5 October 1971.
6. Interview with Lucy Middleton, London, 13 October 1971.
7. Interview with Lena Jeger, 11 October 1971.
8. David E. Butler and Jennie Freeman, *British Political Facts, 1900-1960* (London: Macmillan & Co., 1969), p. 100.
9. Interview with Edith, Lady Summerskill, London, 12 October 1971.
10. A. J. Cummings, "We Need More Women M.P.s," *News Chronicle*, 14 December 1948.
11. Interview with Lucy Middleton, London, 13 October 1971.
12. Mrs. Mabel Philipson, Conservative M.P. from 1923-1929, upon refusing to run again (quoted in the *Daily Telegraph*, November 20, 1928).
13. Mrs. Beatric Wright, Conservative M.P. from 1941-1945, upon her remarriage. Mrs. Wright had succeeded her first husband, Flying Officer J. R. Rathbone, after his death in World War II (quoted in the *Manchester Guardian*, January 9, 1945).
14. Mrs. Joyce Butler, Labor M.P. since 1955 (quoted in the *Daily Telegraph*, March 18, 1966).
15. The following women had fathers who were M.P.s: Conservatives, Lady Davidson, Patricia Ford and Lady Iveagh; Liberals, Megan Lloyd-George and Hilda Runciman; Independent, Eleanor Rathbone; Labor, Lady Noel-Buxton and Muriel Nichol.
16. The following women had brothers who were M.P.s: Conservative, Thelma Cazalet; Liberal, Megan Lloyd-George; Labor, Lady Summerskill.
17. Patricia Ford, Conservative, took her father's seat.
18. The following women took their husband's seat: Conservatives, Lady Gammans; Labor, Lena Jeger.
19. Interview with Lucy Middleton, 13 October 1971.
20. Interview with Edith, Lady Summerskill, London, 12 October 1971.

Chapter 5

1. (Group I) General Elections of 1918, 1922, 1923, 1924, 1929, 1931, and 1935; (Group II) General Elections of 1945, 1950, 1951, 1955, 1959, 1964, 1966, and 1970.
2. Telephone interview with Millie Miller, Labor candidate, 5 September 1974; Interview with Trixie Gardner, Conservative candidate, 4 September 1974; Interview with Margaret Winfield, Liberal candidate, 5 September 1974.
3. Interview with Judith Hart, M.P., 4 September 1974.
4. *Ibid.*
5. David E. Butler and Anthony King, *The British General Election of 1966* (New York: St. Martin's Press, 1966), pp. 211-212.
6. J. F. S. Ross, *Parliamentary Representation* (London: Eyre & Spottiswoode, 1943), p. 148.
7. Peter Paterson, *The Selectorate* (London: Macgibbon & Kee, 1967), p. 9.

Chapter 6

1. The Representation of the People (Equal Franchise) Act of 1928 empowered all women to vote when they turned 21, subject only to the three-months residence requirement that applied to male voters.
2. Arthur Henderson, "Votes for Women! Tory Record," *The Labour Party* (political pamphlet), October 1924.
3. "The Woman's Vote," *The Liberal Magazine*, vol. 30 (1929): 205-8.
4. David Edgeworth Butler, *The Electoral System in Britain Since 1918* (Oxford: Clarendon Press, 1963), p. 145; Maurice Duverger, *The Political Role of Women* (Paris: United Nations Educational, Scientific and Cultural Organization, 1955), p. 147.
5. J. F. S. Ross, *Parliamentary Representation* (London: Eyre & Spottiswoode, 1943), p. 33.
6. *Ibid.*, p. 46. The terms "public" and "private" are used with their American connotations.
7. *Ibid.*, p. 160.
8. Because her appointment was unprecedented, "there was no ruling to cover the question of the uniform of a woman Privy Councillor," according to a leading authority on court dress. "Miss Bondfield's Problem," *Daily Herald*, 11 June 1929.
9. Butler, *The Electoral System*, p. 167.
10. R. B. McCallum and Alison Readman, *The British General Election of 1970* (London: St. Martin's Press, 1971), p. 128.
11. *Ibid.*, p. 77.
12. *Ibid.*, p. 74.
13. *Ibid.*, p. 273.
14. David Edgeworth Butler and Michael Pinto-Duschinsky, *The British General Election of 1970* (London: St. Martin's Press, 1971), p. 128.
15. *Ibid.*, p. 300.
16. *Ibid.*, p. 346.
17. *Times* (London), *Guide to the House of Commons* 1970, p. 256.
18. *Times* (London), 1 May 1945.
19. Ross, *Parliamentary Representation*, p. 116.
20. Peter Paterson, *The Selectorate* (London: Macgibbon & Kee, 1967), p. 48.
21. Ross, *Parliamentary Representation*, p. 231; *Newcastle News*, 14 February 1925.
22. McCallum and Readman, *General Election of 1945*, p. 83.

Chapter 7

1. *Times* (London), 29 November 1935.
2. *Ibid.*
3. *Manchester Guardian*, 16 July 1930.
4. Ethel M. Wood, "Women in Parliament," *Times*, 9 November 1944.
5. Peter Paterson, *The Selectorate* (London: Macgibbon & Kee, 1967), p. 45.
6. David Butler and Anthony King, *The British General Election of 1966* (New York: St. Martin's Press, 1966), p. 267.

7. Interview with Trixie Gardner, London, 4 September 1974.
8. *News Chronicle*, 15 June 1932.
9. Interview with Lena Jeger, London, 11 October 1971.
10. *Clarion*, 12 December 1924.
11. Margaret Goldsmith, *Women and the Future* (London: Lindsay Drummond United, 1946), p. 111.
12. Margaret Laing, ed., *Woman on Woman* (London: Sidgwick & Jackson, 1971), Chapter 7: "Children Are Not the Enemy," by Elizabeth Longford, p. 223.
13. Lady Summerskill, "Ideal Husband, Imperfect Law," p. 134.
14. Melita Spraggs, "British Women Show Purpose in Politics," *Christian Science Monitor*, 19 July 1945.
15. Interview with Joan, Lady Davidson, London, 5 October 1971.
16. Interview with Edith, Lady Summerskill, London, 12 October 1971.
17. Lady Summerskill, "Ideal Husband," p. 137.
18. Longford, "Children," p. 225.
19. Interview with Margaret Winfield, London, 5 September 1974.
20. Laing, *Woman on Woman*, p. 2.
21. *Ibid.*, p. 3.
22. *Daily Mail*, 18 April 1939; *Evening Standard*, 19 June 1939.
23. Maurice Duverger, *The Political Role of Women* (Paris: United Nations Educational, Scientific and Cultural Organization, 1955), p. 124.
24. "Women M.P.s on their Work," *Northern Gazette*, 29 June 1932.
25. *Manchester Guardian*, 1 December 1940.
26. Ray Strachey, ed., *Five Women: Our Freedom and Its Results* (London: Hogarth Press, 1936), Chapter 5: "Changes in Social Life," by Mary Agnes Hamilton, p. 243.
27. William L. O'Neill, "The Woman Movement," in *Historical Problems: Studies and Documents*, ed. G. R. Elton (London: George Allen & Unwin, 1969), p. 25.
28. *Labour Woman*, vol. 5, February 1968, p. 23.
29. Richard Evans, "M.P. 'Hounded out of Public Life,'" *Financial Times*, 26 February 1970.
30. *Daily Express*, 19 February 1961.
31. *Birmingham Post*, 16 April 1968.
32. *News Chronicle*, 9 November 1938.
33. *Daily Telegraph*, 9 July 1933.
34. *Daily Herald*, 29 March 1940.
35. "Women Members in Parliament," *Times*, 24 January 1924.
36. *Times*, 1 November 1964.
37. Duverger, *The Political Role*, p. 149.
38. *Labour Woman*, vol. 57, February 1968, p. 23.

Appendix

1. F. W. S. Craig, *British Parliamentary Election Results, 1918-1970*, Vol. 1 (Glasgow: Political Reference Publications, 1969); Vol. 2 (Chichester: Political Reference Publications, 1971).
2. Times Newspapers Ltd., *Guide to the House of Commons* (London: Times Newspapers Ltd., 1929-1970).
3. *Dod's Parliamentary Companion* (London: Business Dictionaries, 1929, 1945, 1970).

Selected
Bibliography

Primary Sources

1. Eleanor F. Rathbone Collection, Harold Cohen Library, University of Liverpool.
   1. Private Correspondence
   2. Files of Correspondence and papers relating to her public activities
   3. Miscellaneous
      a. File of Election Addresses
      b. File of Circular Letters to Constituents
      c. Scrapbooks Containing Press Clippings
      d. Notes for Speeches
2. Ellen Wilkinson Scrapbooks, Labor Party Library, Transport House, London.
   The six scrapbooks contain newspaper clippings of Miss Wilkinson's career from April 1924 until her death in 1947. She left no personal papers.
3. Interviews
   1. Interview with Joan, Lady Davidson, London, 13 October 1971.
   2. Interview with Edith, Lady Summerskill, London, 12 October 1971.
   3. Interview with Lucy Middleton, London, 13 October 1971.
   4. Interview with Lena Jeger, London, 11 October 1971.
   5. Interview with Trixie Gardner, London, 4 September 1974.
   6. Interview with Judith Hart, Richmond (England), 4 September 1974.
   7. Interview with Millie Miller, London, 5 September 1974.
   8. Interview with Margaret Winfield, London, 5 September 1974.
4. Additional Sources
   For information about the general elections, the party libraries—Labor, Liberal and Conservative—were very helpful. The Fawcett Li-

brary is devoted solely to the activities of women and has a filing cabinet drawer filled with newspaper clippings about the political activities of the Pioneer women.

5. Books

Dod's Parliamentary Companion. London: Dod, 1929; London: Business Dictionaries, 1945, 1970.

Great Britain. Parliament. *Hansard's Parliamentary Debates* (Commons). 5th Series, Vol. 125-824 (1918-1970).

Hesilrige, Arthur, G. M., ed. *Debrett's House of Commons and the Judicial Bench.* London: Dean & Son, 1918-1931.

Times Newspaper (London). *The Times Guide to the House of Commons.* 1929-1970.

6. Newspapers and Periodicals

Birkenhead News, 10 January 1925
Birmingham Post, 16 April 1968
Birmingham Sunday Mercury, 13 October 1934
Bolton Journal, 5 October 1934
Bristol Evening Times, 20 November 1928
Cambridge Daily News, 15 November 1925
Cambridge Press, 15 November 1925
Cheshire Daily Echo, 10 March 1938
Christian Science Monitor, 19 July 1945
Clarion, 12 December 1924
Cumberland Evening News, 6 October 1936 - 14 December 1939
Daily Express, 14 December 1928 - 29 November 1932
Daily Herald, 8 January 1925 - 29 March 1940
Daily Mail, 18 April 1939
Daily Telegraph, 17 July 1941
Daily Worker, 15 November 1934
Dudley Herald, 25 September 1937
Durham Chronicle, 3 July 1942
East Kent Gazette, 18 February 1939
Evening Standard, 6 November 1922 - 19 June 1939
Glasgow Bulletin, 19 June 1929
Glasgow Evening Citizen, 22 February 1930
Graphic, 13 November 1924
Halifax Daily Courier, 20 June 1930
Hull Evening News, 29 January 1929
Lancet, 1 December 1928
Liverpool Daily Post, 9 October 1936 - 1 November 1938
Liverpool Evening Express, 25 November 1927
Manchester Evening Chronicle, 21 December 1928
Manchester Guardian, 13 November 1926 - 7 November 1931

Manchester News Chronicle, 25 April 1941
New York Times, 2 September 1945
New York World, 30 November 1924 - 22 August 1926
Newcastle Chronicle, 31 January 1927 - 27 June 1938
Newcastle Sun, 14 February 1925
News Chronicle, 19 September 1938 - 18 April 1944
North East Daily Gazette, 16 February 1925 - 21 February 1930
Northeastern Chronicle, 15 October 1936
Northern Echo (Darlington), 21 February 1928 - 13 October 1936
Northern Evening Dispatch, 6 April 1927, 10 September 1928
Northern Whig, 31 July 1941
Nottingham Gazette, 22 January 1940
Oldham Standard, 11 December 1924
Patriot, 9 May 1929
Portsmouth Evening News, 17 May 1928
Reynolds, 17 May 1925
San Francisco Examiner, 26 January 1930
Scotsman (Edinburgh), 28 October 1930
Shields News, 9 October 1936
Southern Daily Echo, 2 April 1931
Surrey Mirror, 10 June 1932
Times (London), January 1920 - August 1970
Torquay Times, 5 June 1942
Walsall Observer, 25 September 1937
Western Mail, 12 November 1924
Yorks Evening News, 10 December 1924
Yorks Post, 6 October 1936 - 23 September 1940

Secondary Sources

Aries, Philippe. *Centuries of Childhood: A Social History of Family Life.* Translated by Robert Baldick. New York: Knopf, 1962.

Atholl, Duchess of, Katharine. *Working Partnership, Being the Lives of John George, 8th Duke of Atholl and of His Wife, Katharine Marjory Ramsay.* London: Arthur Barker, 1958.

_____. *The Tragedy of Warsaw and its Documentation.* London: John Murray, 1945.

_____. *Searchlight on Spain.* London: Purnell & Sons, 1938.

_____. *The Conscription of a People.* New York: Columbia University Press, 1931.

Attlee, C. R. *As It Happened.* London: William Heinemann, 1954.

Booth, A. H. *British Hustings, 1924-1950.* London: Frederick Mullen, 1956.

Braddock, Jack and Bessie. *The Braddocks.* London: MacDonald, 1963.

Britain: An Official Handbook. British Central Office of Information, 1973.

Brookes, Pamela. *Women at Westminster.* Foreword by Mary Stocks. London: Peter Davies, 1967.

Butler, David Edgeworth. *The Electoral System in Britain Since 1918.* Oxford: Clarendon Press, 1963.

————. *The Study of Political Behavior.* London: Hutchinson & Co., 1958.

————. *The British General Election of 1955.* London: Macmillan & Co., 1955.

————. *The British General Election of 1951.* London: Macmillan & Co., 1952.

Butler, David and Pinto-Duschinsky, Michael. *The British General Election of 1970.* London: St. Martin's Press, 1971.

————. *British Political Facts, 1900-1960,* 3rd ed. London: Macmillan & Co., 1969.

————. *The British General Election of 1966.* New York: St. Martin's Press, 1966.

————. *The British General Election of 1959.* London: Macmillan & Co., 1960.

Clark, F. *The Economic Rights of Women.* Eleanor Rathbone Memorial Lecture, No. 13. Liverpool: University of Liverpool Press, 1963.

Clemens, Cyril. *The Man from Limehouse: Clement Richard Attlee.* Missouri: International Mark Twain Society, 1946.

Craig, F. W. S., ed. *British Parliamentary Election Results, 1918-1970.* 1 Vol.: Glasgow: Political Reference Publications, 1969; 2 Vols.: Chichester: Political Reference Publications, 1971.

Dalton, Hugh. *The Fateful Years, Memoirs 1931-1945.* London: Frederick Mullen, 1957.

Denning, Lord. *The Equality of Women.* Eleanor Rathbone Memorial Lecture, No. 9. Liverpool: University of Liverpool Press, 1960.

Duverger, Maurice. *The Political Role of Women.* Paris: United Nations Educational, Scientific and Cultural Organizations, 1955.

Epstein, M., ed. *Annual Register for the Year 1939.* London: Longmans, Green & Co., 1940.

Foot, Michael. *Aneurin Bevan,* 1 Vol.: London: Macgibbon & Kee, 1962; 2 Vols.: London: David Pognter, 1973.

Goldsmith, Margaret. *Women and the Future.* London: Lindsay Drummond United, 1946.

Hudson, Kenneth. *Men and Women: Feminism and Anti-Feminism Today.* Newton Abbott: England, David & Charles, 1968.

Kamm, Josephine. Foreword by Mary Stocks (Baroness Stocks). *Rapiers and Battleaxes: The Woman's Movement and its Aftermath.* London: George Allen & Unwin, Ltd., 1966.

Kulford, Roger. *Votes for Women*. London: Faben & Faben, 1957.

Laing, Margaret, ed. *Woman on Woman*. London: Sidgwick & Jackson, 1971.

Lee, Jennie. *This Great Journey, 1904-1945*. London: Macgibbon & Kee, 1963.

Madge, Charles, ed. *Pilot Guide to the General Election*. London: The Pilot Press, 1945.

McCallum, R. B. and Readman, Alison. *The British General Election of 1945*. London: Frank Cass & Co., 1964.

McElwee, William. *Britain's Locust Years, 1918-1940*. London: Faben & Faben, 1962.

McKenzie, R. T. *British Political Parties: The Distribution of Power Within the Conservative and Labour Parties*. New York: Frederick A. Praeger, 1964.

Morrison, Herbert. *An Autobiography*. Long Acre, London: Oldhams Press, 1960.

Mowat, Charles Loch. *Britain Between the Wars 1918-1940*. Chicago: The University of Chicago Press, 1955.

O'Malley, I. B. *Women in Subjection: A Study of the Lives of English-women before 1832*. London: Duckworth, 1933.

O'Neill, William L. *The Woman Movement*. In *Historical Problems: Studies and Documents*, ed. G. R. Elton. London: George Allen & Unwin, Ltd., 1969.

Orwell, George. *Homage to Catalonia*. New York: Harcourt, Brace & Co., 1952.

Pankhurst, E. Sylvia. *The Suffragette, The History of the Women's Militant Suffrage Movement, 1905-1910*. London: Gay & Hancock, Ltd., 1911.

Paterson, Peter. *The Selectorate*. London: Macgibbon & Kee, 1967.

Rathbone, Eleanor F. *Child Marriage: The Indian Minotaur*. London: George Allen & Unwin, Ltd., 1935.

————. *The Ethics and Economics of Family Endowment*. The Social Service. London: The Epworth Press, 1927.

————. *The Disinherited Family*. London: Edward Arnold & Co., 1924.

————. *William Rathbone: A Memoir*. London: Macmillan & Co., 1905.

Ross, J. F. S. *Parliamentary Representation*. London: Eyre & Spottis-woode, 1943.

Rover, Constance. *Women's Suffrage and Party Politics in Britain, 1866-1914*. Toronto: University of Toronto Press, 1967.

Sarolea, Charles. *Daylight on Spain*. London: Hutchinson & Co., 1941.

Simey, T. S. *Social Purpose and Social Science*. Eleanor Rathbone Memorial Lecture, No. 14. Liverpool: University of Liverpool Press, 1964.

Stocks, Mary D. *Eleanor Rathbone: A Bibliography.* London: Victor Gollancz, 1949.

Strachey, Ray, ed. *Five Women: Our Freedom and Its Results.* London: Hogarth Press, 1936.

_____. *Struggle: The Stirring Story of Woman's Advance in England.* New York City: Duffield and Co., 1930.

_____. *Millicent Garrett Fawcett.* London: John Murray, 1931.

Summerskill, Edith. *Letters to My Daughter.* London: William Heinemann, 1957.

Wilkinson, Ellen. *The Town That Was Murdered.* London: Victor Gollancz, 1939.

_____. *Peeps at Politicians.* London: Philip Allan & Co., Ltd., 1930.

Williams, Francis. *A Prime Minister Remembers: The War and Post-War Memoirs of the Rt. Hon. Earl Attlee.* London: William Heinemann, 1961.

Wootton, Baroness (Barbara Wootton). *Renumeration in a Welfare State.* Eleanor Rathbone Memorial Lecture, No. 11. Liverpool: Liverpool University Press, 1960.

Index

ASSAM UNIVERSITY, SILCHAR